SAGGISTICA 9

Italy at the Crossroads

Italy at the Crossroads

Gianfranco Viesti

Translated from the Italian by
Ilaria Marra Rosiglioni

BORDIGHERA PRESS

Library of Congress Control Number: 2013947910

Printed in the United States.

Published by
BORDIGHERA PRESS
John D. Calandra Italian American Institute
25 West 43rd Street, 17th Floor
New York, NY 10036

SAGGISTICA 9
ISBN 978-1-59954-071-9

a mia figlia Daniela,
giovane donna meridionale

TABLE OF CONTENTS

CHAPTER 1

New Words for Italy

Italy has come to a grinding halt. Its economy had already slowed down well before the great crisis; its growth was fatigued and many problems of its society and its economy worsened and eventually went unresolved. A new wave of data and studies allows us to better understand this halt and the probable causes that are at the root of the problem. In its history, Italy has shown many interesting differences with respect to the other European countries. It is a different model for capitalism; possesses a different type of social and economic organization that is not necessarily worse than any of the other countries: quite simply it has its own pros and cons. However, the grinding halt of the Italian economy in the new century illustrates one thing quite clearly: that this model of capitalism and society is having more and more difficulty ensuring the well-being of all Italians in the present and in the future. The system cannot be changed in a radical manner, as some superficial champions of Anglo-Saxon liberalism would suggest; but certainly small changes are not sufficient either. Italy needs to undergo a "special maintenance" procedure.

The great crisis, as with all great crises, could produce radical changes with lasting consequences. Like all the great crises, it comes with its fair share of risky options. There is the option to use all of one's resources and efforts to defend that which one already has, in the hopes of "riding out the storm" with as little damage as possible. There is the risk that one might place emphasis on changing that which is easier to change, and that might be yielding modest results, and leaving what does not work at all, intact. In the Italian public discourse there is a general consensus among the various political parties and the media regarding the need for change. However, when the time comes to delineating how to make those changes and what changes to make, the theories become vaguer. Overall, one perceives that many individuals, groups, and corporations only support changes that will improve their own condition, or that of their supporters, rather than the general condition of the country. It is easy to say that a crisis is an opportunity to bring about change. A crisis is a moment that requires abilities that are out of the ordinary. One must manage what already exists and prevent its depletion while at the same time enact a plan of progressive change: a sort of programmed maintenance.

It is certain that now, more than ever before, is the time for politics to step onto the scene. It is time to have the ability to imagine not an Italy of one's dreams, but an Italy that is different and better. It is time to plan a change that yields its fruits right away but that also has prospects for the future as well. All of this must have the consent and approval of the citizens. Unfortunately, as the results of national elections of 2013 also show, it seems that no one in Italy possesses this ability. There is no general consensus on what needs to be done immediately. The Right focuses on the special leadership of Berlusconi; he is able to once more – as many times was as possible before – accumulate a fairly large share of the votes from Italians, based on his personal consensus rather than his plan of action. He is a leader capable of proposing simple solutions that are readily understood by all to solve complex problems. With fewer taxes and federalism, Italy will enter a new Renaissance, they propose.

This book is based on the notion that these solutions are wrong and that they could very well worsen the country's general state rather than improve it; even though the condition of some will undoubtedly improve at the expense of others in the country, which would explain in part the popularity of these proposed solutions. Essentially, one of this book's fundamental notions is that the "maintenance program" proposed by Berlusconi is wrong, though it does contain some interesting proposals. This book proposes to illustrate to its readers "why." It proposes to take a step further and reflect upon the elements that could constitute a political alternative that is both capable of convincing voters and doing something good for the country.

The Left is undergoing a moment of great difficulty in Italy. This is true in many other European countries as well. This is due to reasons that are deeply connected to the transformations that globalization has brought to the economies of Europe: the changes in the economic environment and society, the difficulties in the role that the State plays and in public policy. The Left appears to be experiencing even bigger problems in Italy. It governed from 1996 to 2001 with great results in the beginning before undergoing a traumatic change mid-way through its term (when Romano Prodi was forced to resign) that damaged its ability to govern, which cost it the trust of its voters. It remained the opposing party for nearly the rest of the decade with a brief interruption from 2006-08, which only tarnished its reputation further. Though it represents a good part of the Italian people, it does not hold the majority. It supported the short (2011-2012) government of Mario Monti, who successfully managed to overcome the financial turbulence in the autumn of 2011 and to stabilize public finances after the "creative finance" of Berlusconi's economic minister, Giulio Tremonti; but, with its austerity policies, Monti was not able to stop the recession and to acquire widespread support of the voters. The Left seemed ready to acquire the support of the majority and to rule the country, but this did not happen. The Right proved capable of maintaining one third of the votes. And a new Populist, anti-system party, led by a former comedian, Beppe Grillo, gained one fourth of the votes of the scared and disappointed Italians.

Why did this happen? One possible answer is that it is not easy to understand the Italian Left's agenda. How does it see Italy in 2030? How do they plan on getting there? On many occasions, the Left appears to voters as the more conservative of the political alliances. It appears to be the coalition that proposes minor changes and that proposes to maintain Italy more or less the way it is now. Perhaps this explains why the Democratic Party has received a limited consensus; the citizens feel the need for more important changes. The Left seems to be the party that, at times, does not distinguish itself from the other alliance as much for the objectives it expresses but rather for the more articulate manner in which it proposes to reach them. Perhaps this renders the differences between the alliances more blurry.

It seems as though the Italian Left is at a loss for words: the words that the great, traditional Socialists and Reformers of the previous century had found and built throughout the decades. It is around those words that the Left had gathered consensus and participation from the people. Those words were the foundation for all of their governing actions and are what made them inherently different from their political opponents. Regardless of whether their actions were right or wrong, they were recognizable. Symbolic. Leftist. Trying to propose words is anything but easy, especially if one is trying to avoid stale rhetoric and setting attractive, but unattainable, goals. Politics, however, cannot exist without words.

This book ambitiously proposes to suggest a few words. The first and most important word is: Work. This is not an original notion, but it is also not at the heart of the political debates all around Italy either. Italy needs more jobs. She cannot be resigned to unemployment or the voluntary exclusion from the job market but rather make employment for everyone an objective for the future. Italy needs full employment to grow and produce more wealth for all her citizens. Putting more Italians to work means raising potential production and increasing the rate of growth. Production and income in Italy could increase after the crisis by following two paths: preferably both contemporaneously. One path would be to increase the value of employment that already exists by increasing productivity. The other path would be to create more jobs. More Italians at work means that the rate of consumption would increase, which would be an indispensable contribution to internal demand in which public spending, due to financial constraints, would no longer be a stimulus. It would act as a complement, a considerably larger one, to the income that the country receives from its exports. More Italians at work would mean that there would be more money for social security to care for aging citizens. More Italians at work means more tax revenues for a budget that is in dire need of funds and that will need them even more in the future.

Work. This word appears to have lost its meaning from overuse. Who would be contrary to full employment? Yet it is decidedly more meaningful to ask oneself why this issue is so seldom the heart of any political plan in Italy. Political discourse in recent years has largely focused upon other issues, particularly on how to reduce taxes. In other words, how to ensure that those who already have a good income, or are wealthy, can enjoy more of their wealth through a decrease in their tax burden. Tax reductions mean less money available for public spending. For many, however, the answer lies in merely cutting the enormous amount of public spending that is unproductive. Curiously enough, during a decade under the Right's government, nobody was able to cut unproductive public spending by very much. Certainly a large amount of work can be done on Italian public spending: its composition can be changed. An effort could be made to boost more productive spending to help economic growth, such as research, education and key infrastructures. Its efficiency could substantially be increased, so as to provide better services to people and better working conditions to firms. Areas of unproductive spending can be limited. But when we come to its overall size, it is hard to foresee a significant reduction without cutting services; cutting public spending in Italy would imply a dramatic move towards neo-liberal policies, the dogmatic ideas that modern societies can be led basically by market interactions. However, in present Italy, it seems as though the well-being of those who have a decent income and employment has more political clout than that of those who are unemployed. In the same fashion, the well-being of medium to high-income taxpayers seems to be more important than that of poorer families.

The suspicion that the issue of employment for all is no longer a priority is bolstered even further if one takes into consideration those who are unemployed or who work far less than they could or would like to. The word "work" leads to some other very simple and clear words: young people and women. The employment rate of adult males in Italy is not much different from that of the rest of Europe if we exclude those between the ages of 55 and 65. The problem lies within those who cannot enter, cannot remain in, or those who cannot remain in while maintaining a level of sufficient salary in a legal workplace, in the job market. Young People. When one analyzes the rate of employment among the youth, the low levels are staggering and worrisome. It was already like this before the crisis. When the deep and long lasting recession hit Italy, the situation worsened. Youngsters with temporary jobs where fired; others, including those who graduated and were ready to enter the labor market, remained unemployed.

The cost of the crisis, in terms of job opportunities, mainly affected Italy's youth. Too many young people, including those with a higher level of education, are without jobs. Too many young people are on temporary employment contracts: they are uncertain of their jobs and their future retirement plans are risky at best. Young people are forced to live with their parents and must postpone life's most important objectives: the freedom to live in their own homes, live with a partner, and to eventually have children. Italy's birth rate is extremely low. This phenomenon is typical of a society that appears to have little faith in investing in life's primary purpose: entrusting our survival to future generations. The lack of long-term employment with basic levels of income and social benefits for young men and women is the principal cause of this phenomenon.

On a related note, Italy's rate of female employment is considerably lower than the rest of Europe. Both young men and women are largely unemployed; however women as a whole suffer unemployment on a larger scale. Italy, like many other European countries, underwent a radical transition in the decades following the World Wars. It went from being a society with defined gender-specific roles (men at work, women at home tending children) to a more open society with more equal opportunities. Social and economic transformations crossed paths. Women entered the job market for personal satisfaction on par with their male counterparts. Families and couples living together reorganized themselves and the roles imparted were slightly different from those rigidly imposed in the past. Female employment is a triumph for society: equal opportunities for all citizens, regardless of their sex. It is a victory for the economy: their intelligence, creativity, receptiveness, and ability to handle multiple problems at a time (Del Boca-Rosina 2009) are the motors behind the innovation that propels economic development. Limiting the managerial class to only one part of the population, the males, not only goes against all of the basic principles of democracy: choosing the best among only half of the available candidates is contrary to the principles of efficiency. This process of integration, however, was never completed. In recent times, it has slowed down and come to a complete stop. Many gauges of society development show that in Italy the interest in promoting equal opportunities has waned.

Young people and women are at the greatest risk in this great crisis, when, job security centers upon the male head of the family, at whatever cost. But if young people and women do not have jobs it is difficult to imagine an Italy that is different from that in relative decline in this new century.

Work. Young People. Women. These words conjure up another word: the *Mezzogiorno*. The issues concerning work, young people, and women are of national importance, but they resonate particularly in the Southern part of Italy, the *Mezzogiorno*. There, more than in any other place in Europe, there is a large potential for employment that remains unused. There is so much professional potential and so much knowledge that has no outlet. Many of the South's young people live in precarious conditions. So many of the South's women have been excluded from the job market and are far from even the remotest opportunities to work. This phenomenon does not only happen in the South, with the crisis this happens everywhere, but the intensity of unemployment in the Mezzogiorno is by far larger than in the rest of the country. This helps us to understand why the issues of work, young people, and women have difficulty finding a place on the political agenda: as stated, many of the women and young people without employment are from the South. The issues of inter-generational and gender-related equality are inextricably tied to the issues pertaining to territory. The young women who have college degrees and are unemployed in Naples, who have the desire and ability to be successful and contribute to the development of the country, are not included in the "development" chapter of the nation's political agenda. They are simply listed under the chapter entitled "The South," and therefore, as we will see, excluded from the real political agenda. If they seek opportunities to be successful and to work they may do so, but elsewhere: in the northern regions, or abroad. If they refuse to leave and want to stay in their own cities, they merely become part of an issue that is almost as famous as it is considered unsolvable: the development of the *Mezzogiorno*. This book wants to at least try, for what it is worth, to put all of these words together: work, young people, women, and the South. They are like different coordinates that are, however, intersected by the same opportunity that Italy has to come out of this crisis in an unusual manner and with more faith in the future.

CHAPTER 2

Public Policies

Work, young people, women, the South. These words evoke others as well. Firstly, they evoke the notion of public services. As we shall see further on, employment, young people, women, and the South can only be partly improved by acting upon individuals and their behavior through incentives or deterrents. This is in part due to an important and indispensable element that individuals may have at their disposal: public services. The welfare and development of a country as a whole do not merely concern individuals (as taxpayers, businessmen, or workers) but also the places in which they live, and the rules and institutions that connect, nationally and locally, individuals.

Italy has a strong need to reform its public policies. It is the public policies, ranging from those that regulate the job market, to the budget and the rules for welfare, to the funding of infrastructures, that increase or decrease the chances for young people and women of finding jobs; in all of Italy and the South. It is national public policy that can orient employment towards gender and inter-generational equality. These policies can reverse the trend that reduces the effective opportunities available to a thirty-year-old today as opposed to twenty or forty years ago, especially in the South. They would at least partly unblock a society that is at a standstill; that offer a few merit-based opportunities to its brightest young people.

But it is not only a matter of nationwide policies and services. The economy and society have both changed. Their organization and the way they are governed are no longer uniformly defined by national government. In Europe there is a trend towards a strong decentralization of authority, power, and resources from national governments, even in unitary States, towards regions and cities. This is what happened, though in varying degrees, in France, Spain, Great Britain, and Italy: a result also of their integration into the European Union. Today, several important decisions are made by local or regional governments. Many policies are drawn up and enacted here as well. It is an inevitable phenomenon in a "post-Fordist" society. In the years of economic prosperity, until the 1970s, the economy was prevalently based on large companies, capable of catering to the people through their mass production. All that these companies required, from various services to training, was found within their structures. They were vertically integrated. Where the companies were located was a matter of secondary importance, save for obvious geographical or infrastructural considerations. Big companies conditioned their surrounding territory, but the surrounding territory barely affected the big companies at all. When the territory was no longer in a position to supply employees, as was the case in Turin during the 1960s, workers were hired from elsewhere.

The present day economy is different. The relationship between the businesses and the territories that host them are more intense and bi-directional. The effect that the characteristics of the businesses' locations have on their competitiveness is notable. In advanced regions and cities, the businesses have no trouble finding highly qualified employees, ideas, and research as well as other companies and universities with which they can collaborate. The regions and the cities have considerably differentiated themselves from one another and have become more important for the economy (Moretti 2012). The same national policies can have considerably different effects in different regions. It is for this reason as well that one cannot govern from capital cities alone. In order to promote jobs for young people and women, everywhere, especially in more backward regions, good national regulations and interventions are not enough. There is room for creating local conditions, variable according to each case, which can allow for job growth and fostering local development. The key to understanding this matter is that both levels of government, the national and the regional ones, are necessary. Finding an agreement between these two levels of government, however, is not an easy task. Finding agreement between two (or more, if one takes into consideration municipal government) levels of government is even more complicated and can cause a great deal of confusion. But national policies without good local development are less efficient. The idea of an enlightened center that is capable of changing the entire country by itself (a notion that is still entertained in Italian political debates) is an illusion. It is both on a national scale and on a local scale that it is necessary to draw up good policies for development.

What is the primary obstacle to job growth for young people and women in Italy? The principal obstacle is political in nature. Full employment, the employment of young people and women, and employment in the South were not, and still are not, high priorities in the country's political agenda. Many public policies, beginning with social security, were designed using the model in which the head of the family is an employed male adult. Whoever did not happen to be male, adult, or employed was never the center of attention (Ferrera, Fargion, Jessoula 2012). This is even truer today, in the midst of the crisis: the main priority is to protect those that are employed, of which there are more males than females, and more adults than youths. The promotion of job growth for those who are unemployed or who happen to be employed with short-term contracts, underemployed or employed off-record is not a priority. The incomes of the male head of the family or the pension of the eldest family members are expected to cover the costs of the young people and of women. The family is expected to extinguish any expenses. In certain areas of the country, female employment is already relatively high and that of young people is at an acceptable level. The impetuous development of the past has seen to this. In these areas, immigrant employment, before the crisis, was growing. The immigrants accept positions that are more arduous with lower wages, which indirectly create (for example, for services rendered to families and to the elderly) the conditions necessary to foster employment for women. Young people are able, though with more difficulty than their fathers, to find job opportunities and income. Or the more brilliant minds simply emigrate, thereby painting the image of a curious country (especially in the North) that imports Romanian caregivers and exports researchers, brilliant minds, and those who are most creative.

These issues have been the priorities of the political agenda of Italy for some time now: to maintain and strengthen the development of those who are already ahead. The "issue of the North": the so-called "*questione settentrionale*," apparently opposed to the traditional "*questione meridionale*," the "issue of the South," about the development of the Mezzogiorno. The "issue of the North" concerns reducing taxes. Since the beginning of the 1990s, taxation in Italy has increased with the emergence of the public finance crisis. With the great recession, and the euro crisis since 2009, taxation has increased even further, especially during the Monti administration, to keep public deficit below 3% of the national GDP, as required by the European stability pact. For a given amount of taxes to be paid, some of which are independent from the business cycle, when the economic situation worsens, the people are greatly affected. But what happens to public services if the government's income shrinks? As previously stated, some Italians just believe that there are a great deal of unproductive expenditures that can be cut. With booming political corruption, and the strong campaign of Beppe Grillo against the "costs of politics," they think that reducing both the number of congressmen and their salaries would be enough to substantially reduce taxation. Reducing the "costs of politics" in Italy would be a very good decision, for several reasons. However, the magnitude of those savings has nothing to do with a real tax rebate for the Italians. Other Italians just do not care much for public services in general. They want to have good schools and roads for themselves and their families; as Berlusconi's finance minister Giulio Tremonti stated in his book (Tremonti 2008), they do not care any more about the status of the national health system; they only care about the specific hospital of their city.

There is a growing consensus on the issue of reducing the size of the public sector; however, every interest group is fiercely lobbying to defend their own interests and services. Finally, a large number of people in the more developed North are simply thinking of reducing public services in the less developed, and less revenue-generating South, as we will see later. The developed North asks, with its booming voice, to be entitled to more of the wealth that has been obtained. If the available public funds are insufficient, one could entertain the notion of transferring via public budget resources to the South. What matters more, it seems, is the well-being of individuals and of territories, not what is in the nation's best interest.

In this situation, the Italian Left appears quite uncertain about what to do. Several times, they have followed the agenda of the Right to gain consensus from the citizens.

While standing before Berlusconi gaining consensus through the use of simple slogans, promising "Fewer Taxes for Everyone," the Left cannot seem to find words to express itself: it is afraid to tell Northerners that Italy might grow if more employment is offered to young people and women, especially in the South, because it fears losing votes in the North.

This prompts us to ask two questions that are political in nature and that act as a preamble to the discourse regarding job policies and full employment. Does a national interest still exist in Italy? Are there any political objectives that are in the best interest of the entire nation? Or is the concept of national interest evermore defined as the sum of the interest of the individual parts which compose the whole: and, consequently, every decision can only be measured according to its effect upon the single parts of the nation's territory or interest group? This question is less rhetorical than it might seem. The political agenda of the Right was characterized by the influence of the *Lega Nord*, a political party that is openly territorial. It was difficult to establish whether the most influential minister of the Berlusconi administrations, Giulio Tremonti, was a member of the *Forza Italia/Popolo della Libertà* Party or of the *Lega Nord* Party: he was officially a member of the former but effectively a member of the latter. In the 2013 elections, he finally ran with the *Lega*. The second question pertains to the time regarding the issues the parties choose to support. What time frame is Italian politics using? One has the progressively stronger conviction that the Right's political agenda, and in many instances the political agenda that regulates the entire country, is rooted in the present. What seems to be truly important is that which the citizens require today. Whatever happens tomorrow, the construction of the entire country's future, is considered far less important. This political strategy seems supported by a large general consensus of the population; it seems as though the

Italians are only interested in the present. They are skeptical of, disillusioned by, and disinterested in the future.

Will Italian politics be able to dust off the concept of a national interest and use it as the basis for decision-making? This risks causing further hemorrhaging of votes towards various parties and movements that are territorially-oriented or who aim to defend specific interests. Convincing the Italians to cheer for Italy and not for their own neighborhoods might not be so simple. If the national interest evolves working over a long period of time, to reach a future that is possible, though not immediate (it is an Italy that we would like to have in ten or twenty years), it risks coming off as a fairy tale that is neither credible nor sustainable. However, it is sufficient to look back to the past to find an Italian ruling class that was credible and prestigious because it proposed an ambitious outlook on the future. Perhaps it is right in the midst of a crisis that taking such a risk is justifiable.

CHAPTER 3

Deep-rooted Problems

This international crisis found Italy in an even more difficult situation with respect to the other countries in Europe, and produced effects that were considerably worse.

This is due to four specific reasons. The first is strictly
economic. Italy has suffered the crisis more than other European countries, with the exception of Greece and Spain. The
drop in its GDP since 2008 has been much larger than the EU
average. However, it is the data pertaining to the entire decade that proves worrisome: Italy is not keeping pace with
the rest of "Old" Europe, and especially with Germany and
Northern Europe, in terms of economic growth. Italy is also
losing considerable ground with respect to the new Eastern
Europe. Why this occurs is not entirely clear (Brandolini-
Bugamelli 2009). Many call into question some features of
Italian capitalism, such as the very small average size of its
firms or the modest amount of research and technological
innovation. These features, however, existed prior to the crisis and characterized Italy in the past, when the country obtained significantly better results. Others refer to all of the
changes that have occurred on a global scale and Italy's
place in that scheme. The Euro, for example, has taken away
the competitive edge that firms gained in pricing exports.
China has emerged onto the global market with products
that compete with Italy's, more so than that of other countries: they are specialized in the production of consumer
goods. The diffusion of new information technologies, for a

series of reasons, was not as successful as elsewhere in the world.

In the middle of the decade, some interesting signs of reaction began to emerge from many, though not all, Italian businesses. Italian capitalism has a thousand resources. One must be very cautious before predicting its decline. It is not an inferior, incomplete, or slower form of capitalism as compared to the one and only "right" form of capitalism: the Anglo-Saxon form. Quite simply, it is different. In this diversity there are strengths. For example, in Italy, the financial system fared better than that of many other countries during the crisis. The banking system required little external intervention. There are, however, weaknesses as well. In a changing international economic scenario, they have clearly played a role.

The second reason for Italy's increased hardship during this crisis is well known. The country's strong development, particularly during the 1970s and 1980s, occurred while consuming more public funds than were actually available. Tax rates were too low with respect to public spending during those years and too low to compensate for future obligations (pensions) (Rossi 2008). This has earned Italy the top position for the largest debt/GDP ratio in Europe (apart from Greece), and implies a substantial flow of interest payments every year. In the beginning of the 1990s, thanks to the determined actions of people such as Giuliano Amato, Carlo Azeglio Ciampi, and Romano Prodi, Italy was able to halt that growth. The debt/GDP ratio actually began to shrink. But then this virtuous cycle was interrupted. Today Italy, thanks to the crisis as well, has a debt/GDP ratio that is worse than it was twenty years ago. We need to include more information in addressing this issue. One must remember that even though Italy's public debt is large, its private debt is considerably lower, as compared to others. Italian families possess a considerable amount of wealth (firstly in real estate, but also in bonds and securities), all due to their (past) penchant for saving.

The third reason for Italy's increased difficulty is the fact that there is more inequality in its development than in any other EU country. In introducing this topic, it is necessary to underscore that a society with less equality is worse than a society whose opportunities are spread in a more homogeneous manner (Stiglitz 2012). A good number of Italians (an increasing amount, though less than in the Anglo-Saxon countries), on the contrary, retain that inequality is only the result of different abilities and a varying amount of effort. It is viewed as an automatic and undeniable consequence of capitalism: whoever is poor, needs to bear that burden alone without unloading those extra costs on the rest of society.

Inequality in Italy has many different facets. Certainly, there is inequality amongst individuals. Statistics show that the distribution of income in Italy is less homogeneous that that of other European countries. There are poor families; fortunately not a large amount, but still a significant amount for a country that is so wealthy. A statistic that is even more serious is that, before the crisis, one out of every four Italian minors was at risk for poverty; this is a very worrisome condition because the poverty of minors is more intense and persistent (Ferrera 2008). This means that 2.5 million Italian children live in conditions of material lack and are often lacking in the social and cultural realms as well. These are children who are laden with a disadvantage for which they are not responsible. In the past twenty years or so, the Italian social ladder has changed: employees in general, particularly teachers, white-collar workers, and factory workers have managed to fall down a few rungs. All of those who are self-employed and those who were already wealthy (including those who possessed properties) managed to climb a few rungs. Certainly there is inequality between men and women in politics, society, economy, employment, and in opportunities in general. This is truer in Italy than in other countries. There is certainly inequality between the young and the old. Italy is not a place for young people, to paraphrase the Coen brothers, and this is quite worrisome. Young people must wait a very long time before being able to afford leaving the home of their parents (the time is identical both in the wealthier North and in the poorer South and is increasing rapidly with respect to the past). Their employment is precarious and therefore they have fewer opportunities, amongst the lowest rates in Europe, to start a family and finding a home (especially if it must be rented). They have less of a chance to be able to afford to have children. The average salary of those in their 20s at the beginning of the 90s was 20% lower than their older employed counterparts. In 2005, the difference reached 33% (Del Boca-Rosina 2009). With the crisis, the difference has increased. One's entrance into a professional field, a university, and in general to the ruling class occurs later with respect to the past and with respect to other European countries. Italian youngsters are setting skeptical about country. Between the elections of 1994 and 2006, the percentage of youths between the ages of 20 and 25 that abstained from voting went from 8.9% to 17.1%. This is a significant increase with respect to the other age ranges (Livi-Bacci 2008). There is inequality between the North and the South. What is even more troubling about inequality in Italy is not its degree or persistence, but its dynamic in recent years and, possibly, in the future.

To make matters even worse, all of this seems to go along with the fourth, and final, reason for all of this difficulty: the great skepticism of the Italian people. Many Italians do not believe that their country can change. They are uninterested in politics. They are interested in their own personal matters and that of their respective families. This attitude is understandable given the prospects that have been announced over the past twenty years that have never come to fruition. The percentage of people who believe that their "main responsibility is towards their own personal family and children and not towards the greater good of the country" went from 9% to 35% during the period of time from 2001 to 2009 (Mannheimer-Natale 2009).

Italy's real troubles are not only in its GDP or in its export market shares. Italy is in the worst position in all of Europe in several key aspects (Del Boca and Rosina 2009): lower levels of female employment, the lowest rates of employment among females who have small children, the highest average age among females entering motherhood, the lowest average number of children per woman, the lowest percentage of young women (between ages 18-34) who live with a partner, and the highest percentage of young people (between ages 25-29) who still live with their parents despite finishing their studies and finding employment. Furthermore, the Italian population has the highest percentage of people over the age of 65 and the lowest percentage of people under 25. One out of every five women, amongst those born in the 1960s, has no children. Italy has gone from a birth rate of one million, in 1964, to half a million at the turn of the last century. "In order to find a comparable birth rate, we must go back to the first half of the 1800s, when the population was one-fourth of what it is today and the women were four times as prolific" (Livi Bacci 2008).

The international crisis found Italy in this condition. This is the worst crisis, in terms of global diffusion and intensity, since the one in the 1920s. Its outcome and duration are entirely unpredictable. Its unpredictable nature, does not justify rampant pessimism, but rather obliges us to formulate evaluations and proposals with the understanding that much about the future, both long and short-term, is unknown.

CHAPTER 4

A Lost Decade

How is Italy responding to the crisis? What paths have the Berlusconi (2008-2011) and the Monti (2011-2013) administrations chosen for the country? Berlusconi has done little to improve the conditions of the country and in particular to address the issues previously listed. He has implemented a true Right-style government trying to allocate available resources towards those who are already wealthy. This was in part the case for his 2001-06 administration, but is even truer regarding the period from 2008-2011. Naturally, this is not to claim that the country's problems, or at least the part that we are discussing, have been caused by these administrations: the problems are deeply rooted in Italy's past. A good amount of Italians is conscious of this, even though there are still some who remain convinced that the country's problems have been caused by Berlusconi and that a change in government would have been sufficient to rectify everything. This is certainly not the case.

The Berlusconi government behaved like a company that has invested all of its resources in advertising and marketing (which is even more efficient when one has control of a good share of televised media, as Silvio Berlusconi has). It appeared to be less concerned with investing in production or research to improve the product known as the "country." While this attitude guarantees an immediate consensus, it also worries anyone who poses any questions pertaining to the future. In the Italian Center-Right Alliance, many contrasting powers have co-existed and continue to co-exist. Some of these have put forth interesting theses that take into account the best interest of the entire country, including its youth.

However, Italy was not governed by Aznar or Merkel. There was a government strongly rooted in the decisions of a single leader. It is for this reason that it is not easy to describe its actions, especially in such a short space. There were no large-scale programs catering to the best interest of the nation. There was one boss. In this administration's political agenda, the priorities established by the leader took precedence over the others. This is not merely relevant as a notion in and of itself, but also because it conveys an underlying message to all Italians: "Do what I am doing. Safeguard your own personal interests and try to work around or change the rules that you do not like. Grow wealthy." In this manner, the new Italian "miracle can happen." As Piero Ignazi writes (2009) that there emerges "the idea of a disorderly society that has anarchic and wild aspects, in which one implicitly acts in his/her own interest, "against" others, which need not be obstructed in order to reach a state of *"enrichissez vous"* – an objective that is, under certain aspects, "liberating." The State itself must be reorganized or at the very least stepped over if it is in contrast with an individual's drive to accomplish something." The alliance of the Right with the *Lega* Party adds yet another variable to this discussion: territory. What matters, and comes first are the interests of the Northern part of the country, the so-called *Padania* area. The *Lega* Party's main objective has always been to openly fight to obtain as many resources as possible for the *Padania* area. They have done so by supporting the reduction of taxes and changing the criteria for the distribution of public spending. They have also supported decidedly discriminatory interventions. In Italy there has been a political party running the country that openly promotes the interest of one portion of the country to the detriment of the other parts. It is geared towards redirecting public spending to the benefit of its voters. The thoughts and actions of Giulio Tremonti, represented, with intelligence, a synthesis between the Lega Nord leader, Umberto Bossi and Berlusconi. It was a form of thought, centered on individuals and small communities (but not all small communities, just "theirs"), and rooted in a belief in God. It is a country of families, as Tremonti has illustrated in his book *La paura e la speranza* (2008). It is an original fusion of many current streams of thought.

During Berlusconi's government, Italy has faced the crisis with an ambivalent attitude. On one hand, it has been a revolution of words. On the other hand, its results have been more conservative. Little is needed to describe the revolution of words. There has not been one political speech that has not underlined the urgent need for "reform." These reforms need to be radical in nature in order to modernize the country. Yet there is no trace of any "reform," unless one wants to consider the provisions that have struck the public education system as "reforms." It would later be said that the University system, together with the rest of the Italian scholastic system, undoubtedly needed major changes. But can a mere cutting of funds, in a procedure outlined by Tremonti and enacted by the Minister for Education, Maria Stella Gelmini with particular zeal, be considered a "reform"? Overall, the government has issued its response to the crisis with an attitude reminiscent of the saying "the night will pass." It has not put forth any significant economic stimulus plan in 2008-09, unlike all of the other European countries. For example, it has not enacted at the beginning of the crisis any fiscal stimuli, such as a speedy plan of intervention on infrastructures, not even any of small a caliber, as was done in 2009-10 in Spain and France. This was not done even to counter the dangerous drop in investments for infrastructures in the past years, in particular on the part of local government bodies that have been greatly affected by the crisis. It has tried to sway public opinion by offering statistics that showed they had allocated funds. In the end, it came to light that no additional public funds had actually been allotted towards improving the economy: the funds that had appeared in the statistics were always the same funds, and not additional ones. The Berlusconi government tried to diffuse a sense of optimism amongst the population. For many reasons, this is opportune on the part of the party in power in a moment when expectations and the general "feelings" of workers are so important. It is, however, a dangerous tactic when this optimism is not based on facts or actions and therefore risks to be relegated to the realm of rhetoric. The government only acted to defend existing jobs by granting extended unemployment benefits and covering wages for companies in financial difficulty.

Instinctively, who would be contrary to political measures that defend jobs and that, in part, defend the salaries of workers in addition to helping businesses stay out of bankruptcy for the time necessary for the crisis to pass? If one reasons for a moment, a few doubts, and they are not small, come to the surface. They were trying to freeze Italy's system of production to what it was in in 2008 by defending jobs by saving, where possible, all businesses and by supporting, even in local communities, the defensive policies that "cater to the industries." They also opposed environmental policies in order to save funds. But great crises, with all of their related damage, also produce positive long-term effects because of their asymmetrical influences: it is because they impose a selection among the businesses and allow for those who are stronger, and more capable of reorganizing themselves to survive and to grow when the crisis ends. It is with those same resources spent on protecting existing jobs (and therefore those present in less efficient businesses as well) that one can protect workers, even if less efficient businesses are forced to close. One can attempt to relocate these workers and to make an attempt to help the best businesses grow. All of this is not easy to accomplish, but it just might be worth the effort. This was not even attempted. The government waited for the rest to happen by itself. It had hoped that since the crisis came from abroad that its solution would as well, taking the form of an increase in international demand which would have increased Italian exports and which would progressively re-launch the economy. This is what they hoped would happen, and that it would do so quickly.

In part, those decisions were justified by Italy's financial situation: how can one even think about implementing expansive fiscal policies with a debt like ours? The risk of State "bankruptcy," as demonstrated by Argentina in the past and Greece more recently, is one that cannot be ignored. At the same time, however, the decision to do nothing is quite risky. What really matters is not the public debt in monetary terms, but rather its relation with the country's production, the debt/GDP ratio. Doing nothing does not increase the numerator (which grows increasingly anyway due to the decrease of tax revenue), but does not counter the reduction of the denominator either. This is a financial policy bent on waiting for risks to considerably worsen the debt/GDP ratio. Too little attention was paid to the long-term sustainability of the deficit in a country that was not growing.

The issue of employment was not the Berlusconi administration's main concern. All emphasis was placed on reducing taxes. In other words, emphasis was placed on rewarding taxpayers, and more specifically, the wealthiest of those. The proposals that Berlusconi's coalition have put forth always aim to reduce the higher-level taxes, the ones that only those who earn the most money actually pay. There is no trace, neither in documents nor in concrete actions (besides the so-called "social card," which yielded modest results) of initiatives in favor of the poorest Italians: those Italians that cannot afford to pay taxes because their income does not allow them to do so. National funding for social policies (poverty, family, gender equality, young people, long-term care) was reduced from 2.5 billion euro in 2008 to 229 million in 2012. In the entire first decade of the 21st century, the goal was the same. The famous 2001 "Contract with the Italian People" signed by Berlusconi on television guaranteed tax relief.

From 2001-06, the Government abolished the inheritance tax: an essential instrument to guarantee less of a difference in the starting point of a country's citizens. When it returned to power in 2008, the administration abolished the housing tax for wealthier taxpayers. What is wrong with abolishing this tax? It was a risky move for public finance and resulted in a significant decrease in revenues just as the international crisis loomed nearby. A fundamental resource for local governments was subtracted in the same crucial moment that a system of financial federalism was being implemented. The most important aspect of this reform can be seen in its redistributive effect: the funds came from all of the taxpayers and went only to property owners. This is not only a matter of wealthy families: there are many middle class families who, in the Italian tradition, have invested a good part of their family's wealth in the family's prime property. However, there are neither poor families that do not own homes nor anyone that rents a home who received any benefit from this reform. This amounts to approximately one-sixth of all Italian families. Others that were excluded from the benefits of this reform include those who would like to purchase a home: young couples, citizens that move from one city to another, university students, and those workers that take on their first job and are forced out of their native cities either out of necessity or to gain experience. For all of these citizens, a tax reform that took into consideration rental contracts would have made a huge difference, and it has been an example set by many other European countries. No offense to the higher class property owners, but is this really the segment of the population that is in the most need of a tax reform? Certainly not.

Another fiscal reform that the Berlusconi administration made, which is also very interesting in terms of its political approach, was the abolition of taxes on overtime wages. In simple terms, it is a reduction of the cost of additional work done by those who are already employed. It is a measure that is to be paid for by all taxpayers in favor of businesses and a portion of workers. Much like the abolition of the housing tax, this decision may seem difficult to contest. What harm is there in offering a tax break to those who own a home or those who work overtime? The point is that by deducting taxes on overtime wages, one offers businesses an incentive not to hire new personnel: the additional work done by an extra employee winds up costing more than additional work done by an already existing employee. This means another obstacle in the hiring of young people. It means rewarding workers that are able to work beyond the required hours: in other words not those who must pick up their children at school, organize a family-life, and take care of the elderly or those with difficulty. It is difficult to believe that women would be amongst those who would benefit from this reform. This is yet another measure done in a fully traditional Italian style: this decision was in favor of employed male adults, primarily located in the North. With the amount of money that this reform cost, one could have abolished taxes on the expenses of families with children where mothers work (or could work) and purchase services. Yet all these this decisions met with little political opposition. Perhaps this was due to the notion that it would be best not to anger the beneficiaries and that it would be too difficult to explain to the citizens that the majority would not benefit from this reform.

The reform that truly defined this administration, however, was the fiscal "shield" for reimporting capital from abroad. The positive aspect of this decision is a generous amount of tax revenue just in time to assist the budget in the middle of the crisis. Why criticize this reform when it allowed for the retrieval of a significant amount of funds from outside the country? The answer is quite simple. Yet again, this reform is a pardon. It is a measure that rewards and pardons those who have evaded taxes in the past and allows them to redeem themselves by making an anonymous deposit. In this case, the reform assists the worst evaders: those members of society that are among the wealthiest who smuggled vast sums of money abroad. This reform guaranteed them safety from future audits and granted them exemption from paying for their past actions. These included profits obtained from legitimate activity, but which then become illegal due to evasion as well as those profits obtained from illegal activities from the start. It was a great reward for great tax evaders. This reform, like all rewards given to tax evaders, sends a clear message to all Italians: being a good taxpaying citizen is not necessary and the risk connected to wrong behavior is always minimal. Minister Tremonti was honored by the Italian economic newspaper *Il Sole 24 Ore* as 2009 Man of the Year. Moreover, measures, like the elimination of traceability of the fees of self-employed professionals, which was immediately passed by the government, could easily encourage tax evasion. It would certainly not be surprising, given the psychological state and political climate in the country, that more and more Italians were becoming increasingly less inclined towards carrying out their fiscal duties. The final sentencing of Silvio Berlusconi for tax evasion, in the summer of 2013, can truly mark the end of an era.

The notion of fewer taxes for everyone sounds very good to the ears of the Italian population. The only way to at least partially balance the State's financial situation is to reduce spending. For many Italians, this is an easy operation: there are a significant amount of unproductive expenses. Are we or are we not the country of "castes" (Rizzo-Stella 2007)? It would be sufficient to reduce the costs incurred by politics and cut the myriad useless and unproductive administrative jobs in order to save a great deal of funds. Is it indeed so easy to guarantee the Italian people the services that they are accustomed to receiving with markedly fewer resources? Not at all. This does not mean that there are no margins of saving to be had from making cuts in the public administration, that there are no wasted funds to recuperate, that it is not possible to simplify and save at the same time, that it is the duty of the country to reduce the costs of the public administration and the extremely large number of Italians that live off politics as a profession. However, obtaining these savings is not a simple matter. It implies a smart spending review: an intelligent and progressive re-organization of the public institutions and carefully streamlining them. It requires an ongoing process of experimentation, monitoring and evaluation. Time, political courage, and an iron will to reach the desired result are required. This is an operation that must be executed with a scalpel, and not an ax; it requires contemporaneous efforts in investment and modernization of the public administration and must begin with the diffusion of new technology.

The path that Berlusconi chose was a different one. National public services have suffered this approach the most. The healthcare system has suffered due to the budget cuts. This is a problem because the healthcare system is facing the rising costs of the country's aging population and the availability of more sophisticated and efficient medicines and cures. The evidence is damning. There are certainly funds that can be recuperated in the healthcare system: acting on specific expenses, procedures, and contracts. Cutting without reforming is easy; but it gets no results. Berlusconi successfully brought a frontal attack on the educational system. He drastically cut the funds allotted towards universities to the point that it is now difficult for many of them to guarantee the salaries of their personnel. The services offered to students have been forcibly cut despite tuition hikes. Then the Government attacked the scholastic system, drastically reducing the number of teachers, especially substitute teachers (but at least granting them a small severance pay for their new status of unemployment). They reorganized the middle and high school level of instruction by reducing the hours of teaching, thereby allowing 15 year-olds the possibility of leaving school, having only completed their basic education, as long as they worked as an intern for a year. Italy faces a future with less schooling and without any intervention that might actually improve the quality of its now reduced length. With the help of the media, the government played the role of the one who wants to change, with ease and readiness. Those who oppose them are the ones who want to defend the status quo.

It is worth reminding readers of the caveat that has already been issued numerous times: some of the notions proposed by the Berlusconi governments are commendable. For example, it is commendable to want to rationalize and reorganize secondary education. Much, however, is based upon appearances: Minister Gelmini's evaluation of the university system, in contrast to truly serious evaluations conducted in the rest of the world, was based on criteria that were not previously established. These criteria were merely announced once the evaluation was over and not at the beginning. The entire evaluation was not aimed to trigger a process of general improvement of the system as a whole. It is therefore not a coincidence that first the Minister of Economy decided upon which cuts to make and then the Minister of Education put together a few proposals to enact those cuts. In this manner, Italy manages to move in precisely the opposite direction with respect to the other important countries in Europe. France, among its main measures to emerge from the crisis, has announced a large-scale bolstering of the university system and scientific research sector. A few words best describe the nature of the attack upon national public services: the general sense of annoyance that public services trigger, and the general sense of annoyance towards anything "national."

The great historical novelty implemented by the Berlusconi administration was actually one that is little known, and therefore discussed the least. The primary instrument used to face the crisis has been an enormous territorial transfer of funds: from the South towards the rest of the country. We are not merely speaking of the territorial effect of the measures which we have addressed thus far: in the South there are more families that rent homes, fewer workers that work overtime, fewer wealthy people that have exported their profits elsewhere (with the exception of the *mafia* and the *'ndrangheta*), and more students. We are speaking of decisions made regarding funds destined toward public investments (tangible, like infrastructures and intangible like research) or in encouraging private investments, to modernize the country and make it more competitive on a global scale (Viesti 2009). Here, we can remind readers that, as far as the *Mezzogiorno* is concerned, aside from regularly available funds allotted for ministries and regional and local governments, there are also additional allocations available.

These were called *Fas* (*Fondi per le aree sottoutilizzate)*, Funds for Underdeveloped Areas. Their territorial distribution has been established according to law: 85% is allotted to the eight regions in the South and 15% is allotted to the regions in the Center and North. This decision was accepted by both the Center-Right and Center-Left Alliances. These funds are tightly bound to the European Union's funds allotted for structural development, to which they are added. Why do these funds exist? In theory, they are supposed to guarantee the less-developed areas of the country an increased flux of public funds given that their infrastructures are in worse shape. In practice, these funds make up for the funds that would normally be allocated to the South, which are scanty anyway. If we were to express the amount received per capita (summing the normally allotted funds, the *Fas*, and the European funds) the amount of per capita public capital expenditure received by the South is slightly less than the amount received by the other areas of the country, despite the alleged additional funds. It is not a coincidence that the infrastructural gap is increasing rather than decreasing. However, the "additional" resources are more visible than the normally allotted ones (given that they are located in a single fund) and they are organized in seven-year installments (so the fund is also quite large). It is truly a small treasure. Minister Tremonti thrust himself upon this small treasure as soon as he could, though he was particularly careful in doing so from 2001 to 2006. Since 2008, the fund was literally plundered. With the skill of an illusionist, the resources from the fund were transferred and allocated numerous times. New resources appeared from nowhere and were presented as new and then re-allotted again. In other words, they disappeared. Despite this impressive skill, the path that the "treasure" took can be reconstructed. And so we have the numbers: 25 billion Euro disappeared from the fund. In addition to these cuts, the government blocked the availability of the *Fas* resources; this amounts to a loss of another 21 billion Euro.

These funds managed to finance all of the government's fiscal policies. In some cases, the ends obtained were comprehensible. For example, 4 billion Euro from the *Fas* fund and over 2.5 million euro from the European Union's Social Fund supported the increase in spending for the Unemployment Insurance Fund. This theoretically supported the entire country, but its effects were largely felt in the Center and the North. In this case, the weaker regions of the South acted out of solidarity for their stronger counterparts in a moment where the country's economy was feeling the unprecedented effects of the job market crisis. Another controversial measure taken was that the *Fas* funds were used to rebuild the region of Abruzzo after the devastating earthquake. In other words, 85% of the reconstruction funding was given by the South. Perhaps it would have been more opportune if all of the regions contributed to the reconstruction of the Abruzzo region in proportion to their wealth. The majority of the resources were undoubtedly used to cover any disparate need. In this manner, nearly one billion and a half Euro wound up in *Trenitalia*'s service contract, one billion three-hundred thousand Euro went towards national healthcare, nine hundred million Euro went towards covering the increased costs of construction materials, and so on and so forth. The funds also covered things like the cost of scrapping used refrigerators, Alitalia's debts, and the expense of hosting the G8 on the island of *La Maddalena*. The worst abuse, however, was that relevant to the grants awarded to the municipalities of Rome (500 million Euro) and Catania for their budget deficits and to Palermo, to handle its sanitation problem. Not only were these resources for investments hijacked and rerouted to balance deficits of local governments, but they were also exclusively assigned at the sole discretion of politicians to administrations that did not deserve them. The message that the government, and its supporters including the *Lega* Party, was sending to the South was quite clear: well-designed programs and objective criteria are irrelevant in trying to obtain national funds. Only strong political ties are required.

The projects to modernize, improve, and render those regions more competitive were reduced. The infrastructural gap is going to increase. The cuts and blockage of funds happened right in the middle of the strongest Post-War recession. The recessive effect on the already suffering economy was considerable. The television advertisements illustrating the bridge across the Strait of Messina (a project that was halted by the Monti administration) served to distract the audience.

It is extremely interesting to note that this territorially-oriented economic maneuver of the government, though it was the first of its enormous size in this country, did not elicit any particular interest or discussions. The press and the television networks completely ignored it. Some protests were made by the trade unions. *Confindustria*, which also represents businesses in the South that were directly penalized by this maneuver, protested even less. Its President, Emma Marcegaglia, did not say a word regarding the plundering of the *Fas* fund. The maneuver was noted by the journalists of the *Sole 24 Ore,* an economy-oriented newspaper, but the articles were always placed on the newspaper's interior, never on the front page. These articles apparently did not deserve more visibility and comments. The world of politicians did not react either. The Southern members of the Center-Right alliance, with the exception of a few Sicilian politicians, said nothing. However, the Center-Left also remained comparably silent, at least at the national level.

CHAPTER 5

A Time of Emergency

In autumn 2011, Berlusconi resigned. Notwithstanding his very large parliamentary majority, he was not able to lead the country. His ideas and the actions of his administration were not enough to drive Italy out of a deep economic and social crisis. This was so clear, even to him, that he preferred to leave the responsibility of the premiership. Italy was in a very dangerous situation, with interest rates on government bonds soaring, in the midst of the general crisis of the euro and the European Union. The President of the Republic, Giorgio Napolitano, then appointed Mario Monti as Prime Minister: one of the leading Italian economists and former European Commissioner. He formed a technical government; he was able to garner the support of almost all political parties, leading the country until the general elections of February 2013.

Italy returned to a less extreme leadership. Monti implemented an emergency plan that included raising taxes and trying to reduce public spending to cut government deficit. As one of his first decisions, he enacted a pension reform to increase the minimal age for retirement, so as to reduce pressure on public finances. The austerity policy of his government was one of the most severe in Europe; he was successful in restoring international and European confidence in Italy, so avoiding a difficult scenario; but restrictive fiscal policies worsened the economic crisis. From 2011 to 2013, Italy experienced the worst economic results of its 150-year history; its 2008-13 performance was worse than in the years following 1929. However, also due to the need to obtain the votes of all the parties in the Parliament, the Monti administration was not able to start implementing structural reforms to change the country. These are those "special maintenance" measures to which we had previously referred. Italy was spared this disaster in the direction Berlusconi was driving the country. But the country's structural problems remained the same; the recession hit businesses and families very severely.

The drop in production and in the employment rate in Italy was extremely severe. It is enough to mention that manufacturing production was, by the end of 2012, one quarter below the level it was in 2007. But the crisis does not affect everyone in the same manner; it hurt the young people in the South the most. Many project-based contract jobs disappeared. These are the easiest jobs for a business to terminate but they are also the least protected by unemployment insurance benefits. Hiring levels were extremely low. The reduction of employment was sharpest in the South. From 2011 to 2013, in fact, the crisis was mainly due to the weakness of the internal demand (public and private), and exportation was the only way to increase sales. Southern businesses are more dependent on domestic demand. The crisis was making the core problem of unemployment worse in its generational and territorial aspects. This is not only because there are fewer jobs for everyone but also because its effect is selective. There is the danger that a good amount of families that rely upon one salary, without extra income from properties or investments, and therefore more vulnerable to the uncertainties of the job market, might slide into the poverty level. The effect of such a long crisis on the job market could be of great intensity and could last for a very long time. The level of unemployment could become structural in nature if businesses adapt to the decreased levels of production. One hopes that this will not happen and that the rate of employment will heal more rapidly. However one cannot solve such grave problems with hope alone.

There is an entire generation that risks being kept out of the workforce. In addition to the precarious nature of employment in recent years, a significant growth in the lack of jobs could risk to make this situation even worse. A marked decrease in pension coverage for all the youth continues to loom in the background as well. In conclusion, the employment issues are becoming much worse for the youth, especially in the South.

CHAPTER 6

Full Employment

A better future for Italy would mean restoring a more steady economic growth for the entire country than in the first decade of the new century, even before the crisis started in 2008-09. If Italy does not generate more wealth, it will be difficult to ensure new jobs for the unemployed, more material well-being for Italians in need, the improvement of public services, the ability to reduce taxes on employment, investments in tangible and intangible infrastructures and better schools and hospitals. A higher GDP will not resolve all problems. It will not eliminate poverty. It will not make cities more welcoming. It will not care for the environment. It also will not reduce excessive inequalities and will not offer equal opportunities to those equal in merit. Growth needs to be accompanied by public policies; however, without growth, little can be accomplished.

There are two paths that must be followed to ensure economic growth. The first path entails increasing productivity: in other words, increasing the value of what is produced in a workday. The other path entails increasing the rate of employment: in other words increasing the amount of people that have jobs. Increasing productivity is certainly the ideal path for advanced economies. There is a large consensus regarding the fact that structural interventions are required on the Italian system of production to ensure its growth. Business growth must be fostered. The country must increase its ability to generate innovative products and solutions, and therefore investment in research and innovation is needed.

Effective large-scale measures must be taken to promote competition in the service market. We will not address these issues here, not because they are unimportant. Quite the opposite is true. We would like to place more emphasis, however, on the other motor behind economic growth: increasing employment.

Increasing productivity and employment are not necessarily two different objectives. Increasing the employment rate can also generate an increase in productivity if creative, qualified, and innovative people enter the workforce. Innovation can also make its way into businesses through the abilities of newly hired employees.

However, the days when governments could count on employment growth through instruments such as public spending, increasing the number of public employees or encouraging businesses to invest in State projects are long gone. This does not mean that politics must give up on this objective. It must be pursued with instruments and procedures that are compatible with contemporary societies and economies.

There are policies that can constitute the building blocks of a strategy to bolster job growth in Italy. Nothing that will be mentioned is particularly original in concept per se: the idea is to put together a series of actions in motion in such a way that each one can support the other, tied together by a common thread. There is certainly a need for a policy regarding taxation. Employment is too low also because the cost of labor is weighed down by taxes and dues that must be paid for social security. This is also due to European and international financial integration. Assets can be easily moved throughout Europe in search of lower tax rates and therefore can be maneuvered to pay fewer taxes. To compensate fiscal receipts, a larger fiscal burden has been placed on labor. The cost of labor in Italy is particularly high with respect to the average net salary: the difference between them is over 45%. This makes it more expensive for businesses to hire new employees and at the same time has a relatively modest effect on a family's income. Italy's net salaries are decidedly lower than the European average (they have also experienced a considerably slower evolution). Their level, therefore, does not help increase internal demand. One aspect of the difference between the cost of labor and the average net salary is due to the weight of dues paid for social security. The other aspect is determined by taxation. How to reduce taxation on labor? A moderate housing tax appears to be indispensable and could be a source of tax revenue for local governments. One could increase taxes for wealthier people. A campaign to reduce tax evasion – quite the opposite from the adopted measures of pardons and fiscal "shields" – can, over time, recuperate missing funds; an amount that is quite vast in Italy. Any resources that are recovered from tax revenue could be used toward reducing labor taxes, starting from the lower salary levels. This could be to the advantage of both businesses and workers. It is on those lower salaries that the gap between the cost of labor and the net salary weighs the most. It is by lowering the cost of labor on those lower salaries that we could possibly see an increase in the employment rate. In this manner, Italy may also be able to combat the black labor market, which not only damages the workers involved, but also the nation as a whole. Low-income families are more prone to higher spending: it is this level of workers for whom a tax break could produce a more significant increase in national consumption and therefore give the economy a boost.

There is a bureaucratic aspect as well. In the last ten years, the Italian job market experienced a great transformation. However, as Salvatore Rossi noted in his book *Controtempo* (2009), this transformation was asymmetrical in nature. The regulations regarding one's exit from a job, in other words those regarding the already employed, remained essentially unchanged. The regulations regarding those entering a new job, in other words for those seeking employment and those who are fortunate enough to find it, have changed considerably. In this fashion, many jobs have been rendered "precarious": the work conditions are very different (and much worse) than they were in the past. "The laws regulating project-based contracts, usually short-term, which were initially designed to cater to the needs of those hired, actually gave more power to those providing the jobs. This is especially true in the particularly grey world of the service industry (including the public part). This is a loaded gun that allows the employers to hire neo-slaves (similar to those workers hired during the time of the Industrial Revolution) and simply passing them off as freelancing professionals"(Rossi 2009). Many pay their social security dues without any real certainty that at the end of their careers they will have any retirement coverage. This concerns young people as well as a large portion of immigrant workers. Equity reasons should prompt a revision of this condition. During the Monti administration, a first step in this direction was made. Additionally, while it is true that the needs of contemporary economies render the job market more flexible, in which it is possible to relocate work from declining businesses to those that are growing, it is also true that for businesses that emphasize quality it is important to hold on to workers that gain knowledge and experience. This constitutes an important factor in the company's competitiveness. More equal rules, to contrast the excessive "precariousness" of jobs, perhaps will not increase the amount of work, but they will certainly increase the quality. These would allow young people to have a career that is less dramatically uncertain than it is today.

This brings us to another essential component of a possible strategy to relaunch employment growth: welfare reform. The welfare system is the product of an extremely complex history and a tangled mess of regulations. The system was born in those "golden years" when full employment was close at hand and the welfare safety net primarily aimed to protect workers that were at risk of losing their jobs. From the 1970s onward, a series of never-ending modifications were made. These were mainly made to offer coverage to those workers that were employed by companies that were experiencing dire problems from which they did not expect to recover. What emerged was a system that was characterized by deep inequalities. In the past, these allowed for generous early retirement bonuses for people who are well within their working years, along with modest unemployment compensation. The welfare system remains profoundly unfair. Italy offers no coverage for those who are unemployed because they never managed to find employment, or because they only managed to find clandestine employment. This includes younger, weaker people. In Italy, "passive" political measures, in other words aimed at defending a worker's income, are much larger than "active" measures aimed at promoting the acquisition of a new job. These are all complex issues: increasing welfare coverage in a more equal manner is costly. It is dangerous to extend the coverage without putting mechanisms in place that discourage receiving the benefits for too long and that instead favor re-employment, even through the promotion of measures concerning training and orientation. Certainly it is not a system that can be changed easily or quickly. Yet again, what truly matters is the path that is chosen: keeping the system the way it is and increasing the exceptions to its coverage, or taking measures to ensure equality, so that everyone has the same rights, and promoting measures to favor those who are weakest.

Here we reach the theme of welfare. The imprint of the Italian welfare system is quite clear (Ferrera, Fargion, Jessoula 2012). A peek into its history, which is parallel to that of the social security buffers, allows us to better understand how the system works. The coverage offered to risks connected to old age is significant: this is also the result of an era in which it was opportune to think about guaranteeing the employed, and their families, an adequate pension. The Italian pension was generous especially considering the increase in average life expectancy. Many drastic measures were implemented over the years to reform the system and decrease the risk for public spending in the future. Italy is now in a much better position than other European countries. The downside of having such a generous pension system was the almost complete absence of measures aimed at assisting the poor, those entering maternity, or for assisting the elderly. This resulted in a system where families play the role of the buffer, with pensions from grandparents and domestic duties and care handled by women with no retribution. An experimental guaranteed minimum income was implemented by the Center-Left in the 1990s, but was subsequently abandoned. Even in this case it is not easy to bring about changes. Over-simplified solutions that involve only a generational exchange, in other words subtracting from the elderly and adding to the youth, should be avoided.

There is another aspect that would specifically address the needs of women. This would require the best and largest organization in the country regarding the services and rules that would favor the participation of women in the workforce. The services would include structures to help women with small children (day-care centers) or the elderly (homecare assistance). These could be paired with laws regarding leaves of absence and work hours that could be allowed to better coincide with family needs. Similar initiatives have been implemented efficiently in France to promote the creation of a market of services catering to families. Ferrera (2008) states that working women, in turn, produce an increased demand for a wide variety of services and therefore create more jobs. Such services include assistance for infants, support for scholastic activities, homecare for those who are not self-sufficient, paramedic homecare, personalized systems of transportation, meal deliveries, as well as assistance and supervision with many home-related activities. If the female employment rate were to reach that of the male population, Italy's GDP would grow to about 20%. There could also be policies specifically for young people. One example could be the Newborn Fund and the Endowment for Autonomy that was proposed by Livi Bacci (2008), to counter the effects of poverty and the holes in the education of the youngest members of our society. Initiatives that favor an increase in social mobility are an essential component in creating legislation regarding young people. However, we must re-establish the parameters of meritocracy. "Very often one thinks that in order to promote social mobility it is necessary and sufficient to introduce a more meritocratic system in the allocation of jobs and resources. The most decisive element lies in accessing a series of opportunities that are the foundation of growth and development of merit" (Stiglitz 2012). These include access to a good education and to exposure to social and cultural elements, which foster the growth of certain types of abilities. "This is because talent and merit are not innate qualities but are qualities that need to be cultivated (...) Very often those who are born in unfavorable conditions enter the workforce already at a disadvantage (...) It is for this reason that social mobility requires two conditions: efficient political measures that guarantee anyone equal access to an economic system that is capable of recognizing merit and to offer career opportunities." (Tinagli 2009) These measures must render self-enterprise easier and faster, thereby reducing the cost and expenses for those who attempt to create a career for themselves as future professionals. In order to emerge from the current crisis stronger and more diverse, Italy needs many new businesses, even to substitute the part of its entrepreneurial base that has fallen victim to international competition. These new businesses, if possible, should be based on science, knowledge, creativity, and the environment, so that they might be able to remain on the international market with products and services that are characterized by originality. These businesses can be created by young people, those young people with high levels of education that are tied to the world of research as well as those who are most creative and willing to take initiatives. It is for this reason that it would be most useful to transfer a part of the resources that are allocated to businesses, which are considerable though not as much as they were in the past, from the defense of those already in operation to support new firms. Some interesting ideas were proposed by the Monti administration in the "Restart Italy" program.

What does all of this stand for? Is this a book of dreams that merely contains the parts of Italy that are the least efficient and that one would like to change with the flick of a magic wand? Is this book merely a summary of problems that is unaware that many of the measures it proposes are quite complex and costly? Many of the addressed themes are notions that are discussed quite thoroughly though they can certainly be revised and must be analyzed. It is obvious that none of the political measures proposed is simple. Many would have an impact on the public budget and they require a careful evaluation to determine their sustainability. Others are experimental initiatives that must be evaluated and implemented progressively. All of them require time in order to produce effective results and an accurate design to ensure that these results can be obtained in a relatively short timeframe in order to warrant a consensus. Technical discussions in Italy are of a good quality; there is a great deal of international experience which one can tap. The European Commission's "2020" Strategy comprises innovation and social inclusion and is asking all of the States to set their own specific objectives. Italy may preserve many peculiar aspects of its system while working on its innovative aspects.

Yet there is something missing. In all of these discussions we are missing a common thread. Why implement these measures? What objectives are we hoping to achieve? What country are we trying to design? In the discussions regarding social security buffers or on the measures concerning a work and family compromise, it seems as though sometimes we are missing the conviction that we are not merely addressing single issues, but rather are putting together pieces of a much larger puzzle. The political measures that are proposed to increase employment opportunities for women are not merely measures "favoring women." These are an important chapter in the strategy to relaunch Italy. They are not merely aimed at improving the condition of women, but also, with the increase of female employment, (and of their income, consumption, and the resulting creation of more work) at helping all of Italy make great strides. Italy seems to be missing the words necessary to speak not of the single measures adopted, but of the objectives it would like to reach. We would like more work for everyone and in particular for young people and women so that we might reach full employment. We would like more opportunities for everyone that do not take into consideration one's starting point, personal information, or gender; opportunities that allow one and all to benefit from their talents. We would like more equality in receiving services and in our rights (as well as duties) regarding access to unemployment insurance and in services available for the elderly that are no longer self-sufficient. Italy needs better public services: if much can come from the hopes, desires, and decisions of individuals (and therefore from the incentives offered that stimulate these), it is also necessary to have a network of public services that are widely available, efficient, and of high quality.

In liberal and dynamic societies, it is the freedom and inventiveness of the citizens that bring about progress. However, without proper political measures, this freedom remains a pipe dream for many citizens. It is evident that one is truly free when one has knowledge (having received a high quality public education); when one is not the victim of power that has been misspent on the job market; when one is not exposed to excessive risks in their career; when one can start a family and have children, knowing that these will not be an obstacle to their career.

CHAPTER 7

North and South

The country's problems, and in a parallel manner its opportunities for growth, possess a significant element that is territorially based. In particular, it is in the regions of the South where the rate of employment of young people and women is significantly lower than in the rest of the country, and therefore it contributes less to the well-being of the entire country. It is here that wealth can be significantly increased. Why does this happen? Why is it that the South is a considerable part of the problem and not of the solution?

The answer that is most often offered in Italy is simple: because the South is the South. It is a case unto itself in Europe and the rest of the world. Over the past few years, a very clear analysis of the situation has emerged and it is possible to define it as the "Southern Theory"(Viesti 2013). It goes more or less like this: our country has spent decades making great efforts to favor development in the South. Colossal amounts of resources have been allocated for this purpose. Many different paths have been tried and political measures implemented, but none have produced any results. The South remains unresponsive to development; it is impossible (and history proves this) to create businesses and subsequent employment in the South. According to many, this is due to the lack of social capital in the South. In other words, it is due to the fact that the people from the South are people from the South and act accordingly. Until this fact changes (and it is obvious that it never will) there is no sense to adopt political measures to promote the creation of businesses and jobs in the South. The only reasonable thing to do is leave the market to grow as it should, reduce the amount of territorial policies and see if this shock can bring about change in the collective behavior of the inhabitants.

This theory is simple and is quite diffuse throughout the nation's ruling class, in the political world, the media, and even in the trade unions. This theory, which is so widely accepted by many Italians, has one major defect: it is false. False means that all statements made at the theory's foundation have not been proven by data or facts. But if this "Southern Theory" is not true, then what is the "issue of the South" today? Let us analyze a few possible answers.

The first: the South is a problem because it grows much less with respect to the rest of the country; contrary to what happens elsewhere, the gap only widens. This notion, which is widely accepted, finds no foundation in statistics, except for the latest data for 2011-12, when the crisis hit mainly domestic demand. For a long time the rate of growth of per capita income has been very similar to that of the Center and North and therefore the gap is actually stable. In the past there have been periods in which the economy actually grew more in the South but the larger growth of the South's population left this gap virtually unchanged. In the new century, the trends have switched places: GDP grows (just slightly more) in the North, but this is strictly tied to a large influx of immigrants. Given that now the population in the North increases more, due to the immigrants, the per capita gap continues to remain the same. Its magnitude is no mystery. It can be explained by the very unusual geographical characteristics of our country and by its economic history (Iuzzolino, Pellegrini, Viesti 2012). Amongst other things, a serious interpretational error is often made: from the moment that the income gap has not changed, the South has remained the same as well. Naturally this is not true given that it has undergone an enormous change over the course of the last few decades, which is in parallel to what has happened in the North. Everyone, however, is convinced that the fact that the gap has not decreased is a completely Italian phenomenon. Shouldn't the weakest regions of a country tend to converge with respect to the more advanced ones? This theory was quite diffused in the past, also because up until the oil crisis in the 1970s there was a tendency for peripheral regions to converge toward the most developed regions of the country. In reality, this might very well not be the case. There are many reasons, for which it is those who are more developed that tend to have a greater chance for continued growth (OECD 2009). In Europe, Italy is no exception. In all of the countries, the regional gaps do not decrease considerably. In many countries, (especially in Eastern Europe) these gaps increase. The development of the backward Spanish regions has been significantly greater than those of Southern Italy. There is no doubt regarding this, at least until 2009-10. However, the Spanish transformation occurred throughout the entire country: the income gaps between its regions, between Andalusia and Catalonia, Extremadura and Madrid, are the same as they were thirty years ago. Italian discourse should really try to free itself from the "gap" syndrome. Given the history and characteristics of our country, it is perfectly comprehensible that there are differences, even sizable ones, between its regions. What truly matters is growth.

The second: The South is a problem because it does not grow (it does not sufficiently grow or does not grow more than the North) despite the colossal amount of resources that have been invested over the course of decades, more than in any other country. This idea is also widely diffused and also not backed by numerical evidence. The South has received extra funds to use towards public investments and business growth since the 1950s; from national funds (more considerable) and starting from the 1980s, from the European Union. The problem is that these extra funds were allotted, if not exclusively, in place of funds that should normally be allotted. In other words, while the other regions use what is normally allotted for them by the government, the South must resort to using only extra funds. While these funds are significantly more visible, if one does the math then one realizes that these funds are not greater than the ones which should normally be allocated to the South. As far as the past is concerned, there is a great deal of evidence but no certainties. We have more certainties starting from the mid-1990s, when an excellent territorial accounting system was implemented. If we tally all of the funds, we discover that the total spent per capita for the "development" of the South is not larger than the amount spent in the rest of the country. Actually, in the past few years, the amount is inferior. In other words, the extra funds that technically replace what should be normally allocated to the South by the State are actually even less than what should be allotted. Does this happen in Italy to a greater degree than in other countries? It is hard to compare these numbers from country to country. Certainly the effort that has been made towards East Germany over the past twenty years is considerably greater than what was done for the South of Italy. Naturally one must also take into consideration that the investments made to promote development in the South do not only favor that area, but the businesses present in the rest of the country as well. These businesses are offered contracts to construct what is necessary. They supply machinery and build facilities. In fact, a significant part of the funds allotted for the industrialization of the South created demand for businesses from the Center and the North, especially the larger companies.

The third: the South is a problem because whatever money is allocated, whether the sum is large or small, is misspent and wasted, in comparison to how it is spent in the rest of the country. This is another widely accepted notion that has been promoted by newspaper articles. The truth is far more complex (Prota, Viesti 2012). In general, the efficiency of the South's local administrations is inferior with respect to those of the rest of the country. Certainly, on average, they are much slower and the measures implemented are of inferior quality. However, this varies greatly from case to case: from administration to administration there is a great difference in the types of abilities and therefore of the results. This theme, however, if it is to be addressed in a serious manner, is not simple. In order to make a proper assessment, technical criteria need to be established. However, there is a considerable difference between supporting the notion that all investments made in the South are wasted and supporting the idea that while there are obvious difficulties, there are also interesting experiences to be pursued as well. One must not forget that a significant portion of the public policies implemented in the South are actually also managed by the national government. This is the case of the highway from Salerno to Reggio Calabria (infamous for the delays in its construction) which is the responsibility of the ANAS, a company that is owned by the government and managed by the Ministry of Infrastructure and Transport. The civil justice system is the responsibility of the Ministry of Justice. Unfortunately, much of the evidence could allow one to say that the efficiency and efficacy of the political measures managed by the central government is not particularly better than those managed by the local administrations. The affirmation that equates investments made in the South with wasteful spending certainly does not have enough data and elements that would allow it to become an assumption.

The fourth: The South is a problem since its citizens are poorer and therefore they pay lower taxes than the resources they actually receive in public funds. The current expenditures they receive are also considerably more than what is allocated to the rest of the country. The amount of current public spending per capita on the South, contrary to what is commonly accepted to be true, is actually inferior to the national average. This is largely due to the money spent on pensions and welfare. The expense is similar as far as basic services are concerned: the amount spent on healthcare is inferior, while the amount spent for education is practically identical. However, the funds spent for public services in the South imply a transfer of part of the taxes paid by the citizens of the North. This transfer has significantly decreased over the past fifteen years, but still remains considerable. This stems from the fact that both the citizens of the North and South are Italian. If the North were to be considered an autonomous state then, from a financial perspective, it would be considered wealthier. However, a correct evaluation of the advantages and disadvantages for these two parts of the country cannot be based merely on this flux. While it is true that a part of the salary of the South's professors is, so to speak, paid by the taxpayers of the North, it is also true that a significant part of these salaries is spent towards purchasing goods and services produced in the North. It is also true that a good part of the students that are educated in the South then go work somewhere else. The problem that these transfers pose is their political sustainability. This problem was smaller in the past when constitutional dictates, for example, those pertaining to education, were widely accepted; when in an era considerably less globalized, the internal demand of twenty million citizens of the South was very important for the businesses of the North. Its political sustainability has been reduced to the consideration that (see the previous point) many citizens of the North are convinced that not only does the South receive resources taken from the

North's taxes but that the South will undoubtedly waste those funds.

So where is the problem? The South's condition is one in which the quantity and quality of public services available to businesses and citizens are insufficient to guarantee a process of sustained growth (Banca d'Italia 2009). This issue remains the heart of the matter. The dynamics of economic growth in the South are considerably less simple than in other places. Less economic activity and less local demand make it difficult for any new businesses to be formed and subsequently to grow. There is a need for better physical infrastructures, particularly those regarding transportation and communication, due to the South's geography, so that it might reach more distant markets: more consumers for their products; more tourists willing to visit the South. The so-called "blue banana," the more developed and wealthier part of Europe, extends from London to Milan, very far from the *Mezzogiorno*. Intangible infrastructures of a higher quality are necessary. The ability of the South's scholastic system to overcome the differences produced by its students' family and social origins is quite modest. The healthcare system does not handle the health of its citizens well. The civil justice system quite simply does not seem to work at all. Still today there are many problems with the South's infrastructures: this is yet another traditional topic of the economy of development and underdevelopment. We need better and more modern schools and better and more modern hospitals. But it is not merely a question of physical attributes. There is a fundamental problem with managing all of these infrastructures. Despite the funds allocated for infrastructures, the services available to businesses and citizens are inferior to those available to the Center and the North. The healthcare system in the South not only has fewer buildings and fewer available technologies, it is also organized poorly.

The scholastic system in the South has worse buildings, fewer laboratories, fewer gymnasiums, fewer transport and food services, all while managing a more difficult population. It also has organizational problems; there is a considerable difference in scholastic results from school to school and even within the schools themselves, more so than in other places. There are also problems pertaining to local political abilities and administration. There are even problems with applying national policies. Many airports in the South are well-managed; but the air transport services, which are critical for tourist development, are fewer than in Portugal or even the South of Spain. This is due to the national policies regulating aerial transport that have favored Alitalia's destiny over that of its travelers. This reached a critical point under Berlusconi's administration, in which a law was passed limiting competition on certain domestic routes to favor this private company that was presided over by some of the Prime Minister's friends in the business world.

There is a problem regarding collective behavior, both within public administration and outside of it. When in the middle of the 1970s the Italian Miracle was interrupted, the answer to the South's employment problem took the form of increasing jobs in the public sector. Many administrations became more important for their ability to absorb personnel than for their ability to serve the public. This process came to a halt with the financial crisis in the mid-1990s and public employment, in the entire country including the South, has decreased in the past years. A process of transformation began taking place and there was an increase in the public administration's efficiency, though these results were uncertain in the long-run, and they differed from case to case. On the whole, this is still not sufficient. The function of the public sector in the South and its relationship with the citizens is currently not optimal. In the South, the lack of general and simple laws has become a widespread epidemic, typically Italian. The application of more specific, tailored measures seems prevalent. Irregular behavior in public administration is tolerated in too many instances. From the 1970s onward, a series of improper and irregular, though modest, forms of income support arose due to the lack of a proper welfare system. Some examples include false invalidity pensions and inflated agricultural unemployment subsidies. These all represent a poor welfare system, which is truly the wrong solution to the effective condition of hardship in the absence of measures implemented on a national scale. Similar phenomena can be observed given the considerable presence of undeclared work and other irregular forms of employment present in the South.

When one speaks of politics in the South, often a caricature or stereotype emerges. The impression is that politics in the South is one large market for the exchange of favors in which the consensus of the citizens is exclusively acquired by the strategic use of public funds. This impression helps no one and only further fuels the notion of the South as a hellish place where all resources are dissipated. It almost winds up legitimizing all of those who benefit from the specific "tailoring" of these funds: "everyone here operates this way." Even the South's more recent political history is more varied and interesting. However, there is no doubt that the objective conditions of individual hardship in the absence of universal policies, the modest presence of organized forms of active citizenship, and the mechanisms of selection of the political class determine the vast areas that are prey to the spoil system. The fact that the resources obtained are used to satisfy individual needs renders solving public problems considerably more difficult. On the other hand, how can one imagine that the individualistic penchant attributed to the Italians that we have been discussing not be applicable to the

South as well? How can we think that politics, in the weakest areas, can obtain better results and that poorly designed laws, like the current Italian electoral law, would allow for the selection of a good political class? These questions do not in the least justify illegal actions or favoritism but only allow us to interpret the South within a more general context of the country's problems. In certain areas of the South we find difficult economic conditions, irregularities or even downright illegal actions, the lack of basic services such as the safety of its citizens and justice, and collusion between political powers and criminals. A part of the South is fertile grounds for organized crime to take root. The *mafia*'s control over certain areas of the South is quite strong and it disrupts political activity, life, and public actions. Fortunately, in many other areas this control is significantly lower.

CHAPTER 8

Regional Development Policies

Here is the heart of the matter: at the root of the insufficient ability of the South to generate employment, in particular for young people and women, there are fewer public services available and they are of inferior quality. It is this inferior amount and quality of services that determines an insufficient development of business and their lack of competitiveness on the market. It is more difficult to be successful when the cost of transportation is higher, when less qualified employees are available, and when public services are inefficient. This situation is the long-term effect of historical difficulties and weaknesses as well as distorted political measures. The South is a weaker Italy. Problems and solutions are basically the same. Contrary to what most Italians believe, this situation is actually changeable. From many different perspectives, much has already changed in recent years. Many political measures have met with success: from the marked increase of the rate of attendance in secondary schools to the development of renewable energies. Like everywhere else in the world, there have been changes in organization and changes in individual behavior. However, these changes have not been homogeneous throughout the territory and they have not been constant over time. If, in particular, the second half of the 1990s had marked significant progress throughout the nation, then this considerably slowed down (if it did not come to a complete halt) in the new decade. On the whole, the positive changes that have occurred are insufficient to tackle the fundamental problems in the

South, as well as in the entire country, or even to set in motion their solutions. What remains considerably insufficient is employment.

As has already been mentioned, the lack of quality and quantity of available public services is the fruit of many determining factors. This means that acting upon one without considering the others will most likely not produce considerable results. Even if many airports in the South have been updated and are well managed, the nation's decisions regarding aerial transportation still compromise these airports and only a modest number of flights are available to these destinations. If there is no widespread respect for the law and its regulations, the measures taken against crime can only meet with modest success. If there is no faith in the prospects for growth, people are less apt to give up pursuing individual shortcuts. This means that expecting immediate results from the measures implemented can only lead to disappointment and frustration. It is more important to obtain constant progress that is not reversible and that is measurable rather than to try to change everything in a few years. Italy must break these vicious cycles. Healthcare in the South is the least efficient in the entire country, but the lack of services in the territory allows for the rate of hospitalization to be higher and therefore the expenses of the hospitals take up too much of the available resources. This renders the development of services more difficult. Justice in the South is the least efficient in the entire country, but the high number of pending trials makes it so the time for resolving the issues are long, which in turn stimulates an "opportunistic" demand for justice. The lack of ordinary funds for investments make it so that the mayors must exert pressure upon the regions to use European funds in order to maintain the current expenditures rather than towards the development of new infrastructures that would allow them to improve their condition.

Without an emergency "maintenance" program designed to improve the entire country, including the South, with the same zeal and intensity throughout, one of Italy's main obstacles cannot be overcome: the presence of potential and creativity in the workforce that is present among the women and young people everywhere, and particularly in the South, remains untapped. There is a lack of opportunities necessary to recognize their talent. The "issue" of the South is nothing more than a very intense chapter of the larger issue that concerns all of Italy. A national strategy to increase employment for young people and women represents, at the same time, the primary instrument that can be used to develop the South. If the South manages to change itself, then Italy as a whole would improve its condition. At the same time, if Italy manages to change itself, then the South will also improve its condition. All too often we make two serious errors. We draw up political measures specifically for the South and expect these to change the situation, without taking into consideration the fact that the South is *in* Italy, when it is there that national measures will be felt and it is there where the country's greatest weaknesses can be felt as well. Another error lies in assuming that the situation will improve exclusively with the help of extraordinary measures without improving the normal behavior of the markets and public services. Let us return for a moment to the possible elements of a strategy to bolster employment: one can easily comprehend that their positive effect would be greatest right in the regions of the South. The gradual reduction of the cost of labor, starting with the lower salaries can contrast undeclared work there more than anywhere else and can foster the growth of new, legal employment. The same can be said of labor market regulations that contrast precarious work con-

ditions, for more universal coverage of social security buffers, for a welfare system that extends its coverage to the poor
and the families, for measures that directly promote the employment of women and young people and that offer merit-
based rewards. A strategy that promotes social mobility
could have a great impact upon the South: placing emphasis
on education, offering more opportunities in the job market
for those who do not have anything or who have not yet established a name for themselves; support for newly established businesses. The same notion is valid for measures
promoting competitiveness and productivity. The South's
export capacity, its role in the international logistics, also relies upon Italian foreign policy in the Mediterranean (which
is decidedly weaker and more distracted than that of France
and Spain.) The country's abilities in scientific research and
technology, and therefore the impetus behind the formation
and growth of new innovative businesses, depends upon national programs as much as on the regulation of the university system and by the opposition posed to the "barons" and
those who merely feed off of salaries provided by plum positions. The success of businesses is tied to the nation's complete effort in promoting respect for the laws and of legality.

However, national laws and policies are not enough
(Trigilia 2005). They do not have the same impact throughout the country. There are different social and economic
conditions in the South and in the North, and in the different
regions within them; collective behavior is different; the role
that the private sector can play is considerably different. The
North has been able cope with the weaknesses of national
public services better because it is wealthier and better-
developed and has been able to apply them, or even substitute these serices, better. Given public finance's hardships, it
has been easier to allow for collaborations between the public and private sectors (as was the case for public utilities)

and to develop projects accordingly. It was possible to resort to private funds, or at least in part, for the construction of the portion of the highway extending from Brescia through Bergamo and on to Milan given that the expected flow of traffic presented the means for its payment. A similar project would be considerably more difficult to undertake in Sicily or Calabria.

In different regions, the same political measures might not be as effective. Teaching in schools that have been improvised in unsuitable buildings without gymnasiums or laboratories; allowing trains to operate on tracks with no electricity; insuring electricity across networks of distribution that are incomplete; performing surgery in operating rooms that do not possess the most advanced technologies; surfing the internet where there is no broadband: all of these actions do not produce the same positive effects that the same actions would if they took place in a different context. It is for this reason, which was widely acknowledged by all and is clearly stated in Article 119 of the Constitution, that it is necessary and opportune that a particularly intense intervention take place in the South.

But there is much more to be said. Within Italy, there is a different ability to enact public measures, manage available resources, and properly design projects for infrastructures and subsequently to implement them; different political prowess necessary to manage public services in a transparent and uniform manner and to identify projects for long-term development. There is a different social pressure applied to ensure good government, and a different individual pressure to promote individually tailored measures.

It is for these reasons that a nationwide strategy for employment must be accompanied by good local policies, not only in the South, but everywhere. The development of a region depends on both national and local policies. It depends on the quality of the ruling and managerial class both at the national and local levels. This is a decisive element in Italy, given the move toward a more decentralized government in the last fifteen years. It is an opportune decentralization, but it is still far from operating adequately. It is still quite complex and filled with overlap. It is important to decentralize power and responsibilities carefully. This could be a positive change that could be more effective in the South than anywhere else. It is where the social and economic conditions are the most difficult that a proper implementation of policies that take into consideration the local situation could make the most difference. At the same time, however, it is in the South where this decentralization could have the most problems. There are no magic wands. The rhetoric which states that federalism by itself could make miracles happen, render administrations more efficient, and select the best ruling class, certainly does nothing to help the situation. On the other hand, what also does not help the situation are the nostalgic views whereby a handful of iron-willed men in Rome are always able to make the right decisions and ensure that their laws are carried out.

For policies to function on a local scale, it is necessary to reorganize Italy; where powers and responsibilities are both given to local administrations, administrations are bound by clear restraints, objectives are as explicit as the results of public actions in which both incentives and sanctions are offered, there are technically competent centers that have powers, and national politics assumes responsibility for the mechanisms of selection of the local political class.

What purpose would local policies serve? The history of the last few decades provides us with some clear lessons from which we can learn. It has taught us that it is both unrealistic and costly to designate large sums of money to businesses without first eliminating the deep environmental reasons that render them weaker than others. These may be in the form of incentives or tax breaks. It has taught us that we need to be particularly careful of extremes: of centralization and an excess of local power. Perhaps too much faith was placed in the abilities of the ruling class at the end of the 1990s. Similarly, history has also taught us to be careful of other extreme opposites: the rhetoric supporting large-scale works as the primary force promoting development and that of thousands of projects for local development which only broke down into thousands of other smaller projects. We need balance. While it is a good thing that each territory relies upon its diversity and potential and focuses upon its own objectives, it is also necessary to not lose sight of what matters to the rest of the country as a whole. It is useless to develop infrastructures of transportation to increase tourism in an area where local policies have not developed the means to accommodate tourists. However, it is also useless to develop these means in a territory that is not included in the network of transportation and which therefore no tourist could ever reach. The history of Italy in the last two decades has taught us that it is important to start from the beginning and not from the end: tourism can develop if the State guarantees the security and control of a region; if the ground is secure and not subject to natural catastrophes; if the education system works; if water reaches the area and the sewer system works along with the collection of refuse; if the construction of buildings does not ruin the scenic views; if one can organize a trip by reserving online, with confidence; if it is possible to travel with reasonable travel times and costs. If one starts at the beginning and looks further ahead, a proper mix of large-scale national policies and carefully designed local policies could produce work, a great deal of work for young people and women, and the entire country could benefit.

The dynamics of modern economics make us understand that it would be difficult for the South to follow the same path of development that the Center and the North followed in a different time period. Interesting industrial areas have developed and grown in the South in the past, but it is difficult to imagine that today, in a new international scenario, their competitiveness could rely on lower costs. There is potential that can be tapped. The high quality food sector is an example for which there are many clear advantages. Sectors that are closely tied with the creativity of the youths, including the entertainment sector, are another example. There are sectors that could help Italy to compensate for the delays in the development of infrastructures, such those relevant to data communication and the internet. There are also the sectors that deal with renewable energies that are actually experiencing a period of strong growth. The environmental sector is another example, in which eco-friendly products and services are offered. The hospitality sector also has great potential along with transportation and logistics. All sectors can be promoted, with an intensity that varies according to what each territory has to offer. These sectors cannot be planned, nor can they be left to fate. These sectors must be accompanied by modern development policies that complete and strengthen the way the market operates. This must be done by starting from the beginning, guaranteeing security, justice, education, and health; but also through research and innovation, creativity and enterprise support. As is the case anywhere in the world, if innovative businesses that export goods and services grow (or if one manages to reinforce those many that already exist) a multiplicative effect takes place in the entire economy. New employment is generated in those services for individuals, construction, commerce, and in all other sectors as well. If women and young people work, an additional multiplicative effect takes place: from the thousands of services linked to women in the workforce that have previously been mentioned, to entertainment and cultural consumption.

CHAPTER 9

The South as The Mirror of the Country

In contemporary Italy, it seems as though none of these themes are important enough to be addressed. Political debate and actions aim more to guide the ship with a small rudder amongst the breakers of the crisis rather than changing the ship's course in the direction of an answer to the questions concerning women and young people, education and welfare, and territorial development. Let us further discuss the "issue" of the South. As we said, in recent years there has been rapid diffusion and acceptance of the "Southern Theory," which is simple and coherent. Nothing changes in the South; the gap only continues to grow wider, politics and the economy do nothing if not continue to worsen. The image which represents the South as a whole is that associated with the waste situation in Naples. This is what happens despite the colossal resources that the nation has always designated to the South, which does nothing but pay for subsidies and salaries for all the idlers that there are in the South. These resources are taken from the pockets of all Italians, the ones that work even today as the crisis continues to take bites out of the hard-working population. Why? Because all of the money is wasted, used for bogus projects, or dispersed into thousands of rivulets. As an Italian economist once said during a scientific seminar held at the *Confindustria* headquarters in 2009: Southerners eat money.

The Southerners are Southerners. There are those who state this by using very clear terms, as the *Lega Nord* Party has always done and continues to do. The main problem with the city of Crotone is that it is inhabited by Calabrians. If it were to be inhabited by the pragmatic people of Bergamo, it would be one of the most developed areas of the world. There are those who recall certain international studies: the South is the way it is because it is dominated by "amoral familism," a notion which was proposed by Edward Banfield (1958); nothing has changed, even fifty years later. There is no sense of "public duty," given that, as it was noted in another study conducted by Robert Putnam (1993), in the Middle Ages, the South did not have free city-states. Professor Lynn of the University of Ulster could very well become a new point of referral. He published an essay in which he stated that the gap between the North and the South derived from the fact that the Southerners were less intelligent. This depended upon the genetic differences between the populations of the North and the South. This in turn depended upon the notion that genes deriving from the African and Asian people were more diffuse amongst the people of the South beginning from the Phoenicians and the Carthaginians (Lynn 2010).

There are those who use an interesting and important concept (that must be measured and used with great care): social capital. However, it seems difficult, if not impossible, to explain merely by social capital why there are so many different situations in the South: areas run by the *mafia* and areas that are completely free of crime, excellent schools and inferior schools.

But all of these ideas may lead to dangerous conclusions. In the first place, if the causes of the problem are anthropological, it is evident that things cannot change if not, optimistically, over the span of decades or more probably, centuries. Secondly, if it is true that Southerners waste public money, then it would be entirely useless to implement any policy at all in the South, given that these policies are the problem and not the solution: the fewer policies there are the better off they will be. This is all for the good of the South, naturally. Fewer teachers in the South mean that there will be fewer idlers that waste public funds without doing anything in return. Fewer investments in the South's hospitals means fewer public contracts with their inevitable envelopes full of bribe money offered to corrupt administrators and politicians and less profit for construction companies that are most certainly tied to organized crime. Public spending invested in the South is always excessive by definition. Guido Tabellini (2008) has supported this notion quite clearly: "The transfer of more funds from the State or from Europe to finance infrastructures or other projects actually do nothing but fuel corruption and the spoils system. They decrease the quality of the local ruling class and allow the voters to become accustomed to vote on the basis of erroneous criteria. (...) We must give rise to a turning point for policies for the South. The South does not need financial resources." And, given the great permanent difficulties of the public budget and the serious economic problems in the North and the Center during the crisis, the fewer public resources that are designated for the South, the better off the entire country will be.

These ideas would allow us to solve a great deal of problems. National public spending could be reduced. It would allow for the territorial redistribution of spending in favor of those areas that contribute the most to the tax revenue and that use their allotted funds better: in other words those who would offer more votes to the *Lega* party. These are not fantastic reconstructions. In only a few months, the Berlusconi administration, as we have seen, without any significant opposition, dismantled the national regional development policy for 2007-13. Over 90% of public spending, however, is not there. It is currently spending on healthcare, education, assistance, and to ensure the proper functioning of public administration. There is a solution: it is called fiscal federalism. For years, the *Lega* Nord *Party* (and its allies) has supported the notion that tax revenue should remain largely, if not totally, within those regions where its contributors are located. In the five years in which it was in power, between 2001 and 2006, however, this objective was not reached. But in 2008, this has all changed and fiscal federalism has become the government's priority. What fiscal federalism are we referring to? In the electoral program of the Center-Right in 2008, there was reference to a project approved by the Regional Council of Lombardy. In the 2013 elections, they ran with a program supporting the idea that 75% of total fiscal revenues should remain within the regions of residence of the taxpayers: a proposal that, if applied, leaves the central government without money even for basic functions such as defence, justice, and interest payments.

Once that public spending in the South is reduced, market forces, always according to this view, will solve the problems. It is necessary that the salary level in the South be considerably lower than in the North in order to compensate for the difference in levels of productivity. Companies in the South are not very competitive because the salaries they pay are too high. Therefore, by reducing salaries in the South, businesses would grow. However, it is not important where jobs are created. If jobs are created in regions that are more developed then the only necessary action to take is to facilitate the migration of the workforce. What matters most is that there are jobs, not where they are located. Recently, the World Bank (2009) contributed to this perspective in its Development Report. The main solutions to the employment and the development problems lie within the mobility of the workforce. For a series of reasons certain areas create more jobs than others: all one must do is to allow workers to move where there is work. Intervening upon the conditions of different areas and implementing policies of territorial development do not matter. What does matter is providing people with the opportunity of finding employment. To favor this mobility even further, it would be necessary to create a considerable difference in the salaries so that the prospect of higher gains could prompt workers to face the financial (and human) cost of moving. This solution, which appears to be quite simple, is actually plagued by a significant number of fundamental problems. Firstly, and it appears to be quite peculiar that many famous economists are unaware of this, the salaries in the private sector in Italy today already differ considerably from the North to the South. Recent evaluations by the *Banca d'Italia* estimate this difference to be around 20%, which is more or less the difference in productivity. The salaries paid in the South actually correspond to the conditions of the local job market: they are lower because productivity is lower. Despite this, if one travels East within the European Union, and even further into Asia, the cost of labor is not 20%, but 80%-90% inferior to that of Northern Italy: it is here that businesses are competitive due to their labor costs. The circumstance that in the South the salaries are coherent with productivity corresponds with market logic: it is not a scandal that the salaries are lower than in the North, but this alone is not sufficient to render production in the South more competitive.

Moreover, since the middle of the 1990s there was a renewed increase in internal migrations in Italy. These migrations were smaller than in the 1960s and 1970s, but they were still considerable. Today, as compared to the past, there are more young and qualified people leaving. The strong influx of immigrants from foreign countries, at the same time, is meeting the demand for jobs that require less expertise and offer lower salaries. Even if these migrations represent a physiological phenomenon, they are not the solution to the problem. The departure of those citizens that are the brightest, well-educated, and most resourceful, deprives the areas from which they originate of their prized talents. On the other hand, they constitute a significant advantage to those areas that welcome them, and that receive all of the benefits of their work without having had to pay for their education. Mobility is a phenomenon that has positive aspects if it is the result of a free choice. Emigrants can certainly return home having been enriched by experience and having acquired new skills. But if the conditions of their regions of origin do not change it would be difficult to imagine that these emigrants would return. In other words, only with an excessive amount of dogmatism could one imagine that the reduction of salaries and the encouragement to migrate would represent the solutions to the problem.

What would happen if national policies gave up on creating work where there are more available workers? These regions would become areas, similar to what is happening in certain regions of Eastern Germany, in which the well-being of the remaining citizens would solely rely upon funds from their wealthier cousins in other regions. Who would pay for schools and hospitals? An even tighter cycle of dependence would be created. An even more worrisome situation would arise: "The South is destined to become one of the areas with the worst ratio of inactive elderly people to employed citizens. To make matters even worse, this would happen in a context in which the public welfare system is particularly lacking and insufficient on one side, and on the other, the conditions of financial well-being and health of its elderly citizens tend to be worse than in the rest of the country."(Del Boca – Rosina 2009).

The discussions revolving around the South have reached their lowest levels in the history of the Italian Republic. The

"Southern Theory" serves to justify the idea that fewer policies are implemented in the South, the better. This is presented as a decision that is also ethical, since Southerners waste public funds. It is ideologically coherent with the idea that fewer taxes and fewer interventions of the government are the way to stimulate real development. In this manner, with fewer resources to invest and fewer public services available, the South's condition is supposed to improve. It is difficult to say how many supporters of this theory actually believe that it is true, or if, in fact, that they aren't simply disinterested in what could really happen in the South in the future. That they are disinterested in the hypothesis, which is anything but improbable, that the situation could considerably worsen in the next few years.

In order to construct policies that are true alternatives to those proposed by the "Southern theory," one must seriously deal with the "issue" of the South. However, in Italian politics many (even in the Center-Left), seem to be a prisoner of the idea that any proposal regarding the South that abandons the "Southern Theory," and that concerns the promotion of the South's development, is counterproductive with respect to the North's public opinion; any proposal represents an obstacle that gets in the way of recuperating the consensus of the Northern voters. All too often, in Italian politics, many seem to accept the notion that the economy operates using a system of double-entry accounting and that therefore any intervention made in favor of a territory results in a subtraction of resources to other territories. In this manner, if one shows to be in favor of policies for the development of the South, one fears that they are subtracting resources from the North. Comparing economics to accounting is a grave mistake, and it is typical of those who only see the present and forget the complex effects that each policy generates in the future. It is typical of those who measure well-being exclusively in accounting terms and within the confines of their own territory; a similar error is now also happening in Europe (Prota, Viesti 2012).

Northern Italy is not strong when it is able to withhold as many resources as possible, but when it is a part of a country that is growing. Unfortunately, in an Italy that lacks faith, the words which express fear and close-mindedness managed to take hold of the Italian people. A considerable portion of Italian politicians do not seem to have the strength to use different words because they fear that they will lose consensus. To make matters even worse, a sizeable portion of the North's Center-Left politicians (especially in the Northeast) and a considerable part of the economic and social ruling class of that area that are close to the Center-Left accept, at least in part, the "Southern Theory." Even if it is more convenient to not state it publicly, many members of the "progressive" party of the North are convinced that the battle for the South is lost before it has even begun and that the reasons for less development are anthropological. They believe that the possibility of a positive outcome is severely limited and that therefore it would be more useful to what can be done for the more "serious" half of Italy, which is facing a difficult moment. In this manner, Italian political leaders are often forced to use a different type of language and different content according to where they happen to speak in the country. This does not offer a favorable perspective of the nation.

The fundamental connection between national policies and the South's condition often eludes Italian political debates and policy proposals. On the contrary, "If there is a region of Europe (…) where investing in young people is most necessary and yet not promoted, it is sadly, the South of Italy."(Ferrera 2008). For example, the decisive importance that policies that are truly aimed at promoting social mobility in

Italy could have on the South is often overlooked. Unfortunately, it is very rare to hear a leader argue in favor of a measure that would aid young people, that would break the vicious cycle of exclusion and precariousness that the crisis only risks to worsen in the next few years. They do not argue that this measure could act against inequalities and, at the same time, promote the development of the entire country.

If we keep the plans for policies of modernization, reform, and development of the entire country separate from those geared towards the regions of the South, the erroneous notion that the former are in opposition to the latter emerges. It suggests that the development of the South depends solely upon what is specifically directed towards the South. It confers upon regional policies proposed a wealth of expectations that, for financial reasons, they could never meet. Everyone expects that the funds from the European structural funds will change the South in a few years and will be disappointed if this does not happen (and they will subsequently, and erroneously, conclude that the funds were all wasted).

The Center-Left's political experience had produced, in the second half of the 1990s, a modern strategy for the development of the South. This was strongly promoted in 1998-99 by Carlo Azeglio Ciampi (former Governor of the Bank of Italy and then Prime Minister and President) and was enacted by the Department for Developmental Policies, which was headed by Fabrizio Barca (former economist in the Bank of Italy; in 2011-13 Minister in the Monti administration). Even with all of its errors in evaluation and application. A similar strategy today still offers the most convincing answer to the South's problems, though it would need to be reviewed and corrected in light of what has happened in recent years. It would need to be simplified and focus on fewer projects (Prota, Viesti 2012). But this strategy has never been adopted as a fundamental part of a strong political proposal. To some, this strategy is too complicated and its fruits, in terms of a gained consensus, would take too long to ripen. An evaluation on the reasons why these policies met with lukewarm approval is completely lacking. In the short-lived administration that governed from 2006-2008, the only political measure that emerged was the one that established tax-free areas. What is most striking about this initiative is its willingness to create an exception to the law: it almost seems justified by the conviction that, given the fact that it is impossible to change the South, protected areas must be created as exceptions. This same inclination is also found in several, though infrequent, speeches given by Center-Left's political leaders. They emphasize automatic tax credits and the reduction of taxes placed on businesses rather than the quality of the scholastic system or on the modernization of public administration.

In the face of the daily presentation of the "Southern Theory" and the partial dismantling of the government-implemented policies for the development of the South one risk emerges. That risk is the development of a strong Pro-South political movement: people might begin to accept the notion that in Italy interests are addressed according to territory rather than to political programs.

The crisis is considerably worsening Italy's condition. It risks excluding an entire generation from the job market as well as many women. It risks fostering the precariousness of jobs and inequality. The crisis is putting at stake national public services like the education system. It risks reducing public morale even further and would justify seeking shortcuts forcing regulations to benefit personal gain. It risks reducing the people's hope for the future. The crisis risks increasing the competition between territories and fueling resentment towards those that are accused of wasting already scarce resources or, vice-versa, nourish itself from the egotistical short-sightedness of the wealthy. It risks giving rise to a conflicting fiscal federalism that is based on each individual's desire to acquire as much as possible for oneself. Secession may be creeping through Italy, and while it is not an institutional secession, it is certainly occurring in the country's psychology, culture, and politics. It is a secession occurring in hearts and minds. A lengthy period of economic difficulties, crises in the business world, and lack of jobs can all increase its effects. One hundred and fifty years after 1861, Italy's Unification might be at stake.

Italy has stopped. It is difficult to imagine that it will restart as it is. If Italy does not get back onto its feet, it risks breaking into pieces, territories, and generations. Preconceived pessimism is out of place. Italy is a country full of resources and it has a peculiar ability, as was the case in 1992, to band together and reach difficult objectives right when the difficulties reach their apex. Public opinion can change; electoral mobility has revealed itself to be stronger than it was in the past. Perhaps even because there is a crisis, Italy might manage to surprise the world. But there is a risk that Italy could break. To re-launch the country, we must foster faith and hope that we could be a country that is different, more equal, that has a society that is more open-minded toward the possibility of taking advantage of the human assets that are unused, especially in the South. There are no more grand ideological constructs to foster this hope and faith: no guarantee that the "sun will rise," as is expressed in the socialist motto. Italy needs the will and ability to find new words. They must be clear, comprehensible, and credible. It must truly believe that young people, women, and the South are not the problem, but the solution.

Banca d'Italia 2009
"Mezzogiorno e politiche regionali," *Seminari e convegni* 2.

Banfield, E. 1958
The Moral Basis of a Backward Society. New York: The Free P.

Brandolini, A. and M. Bugamelli. 2009
"Rapporto sulle tendenze nel sistema produttivo italiano," *Questioni di Economia e finanza* 45, Banca d'Italia, Roma. Centro Studi Confindustria 2009. *Scenari economici* 6 (Fall).

Del Boca, D. and A. Rosina. 2009
Famiglie sole. Sopravvivere con un welfare inefficiente. Bologna: il Mulino.

Ferrera, M. 2008
Il fattore D. Perché il lavoro delle donne farà crescere l'Italia. Milano: Mondadori.

Ferrera, M., Fargion V., Jessoula M. 2012
Alle radici del welfare all'italiana. Origini e futuro di un modello sociale squilibrato. Venezia: Marsilio.

Ignazi, P. 2009
La fattoria degli italiani. I rischi della seduzione populista. Milano: Rizzoli.

Iuzzolino G., Pellegrini G., Viesti G. 2012
Convergence among Italian Regions 1861-2011. Economic History Working Paper n. 22. Rome: Bank of Italy.

Livi Bacci, M. 2008
Avanti giovani, alla riscossa. Come uscire dalla crisi giovanile in Italia. Bologna: il Mulino.

Lynn, R. 2010
"In Italy, North-South differences in IQ predict differences in income, education, infant mortality, stature, and literacy," *Intelligence* 38: 93-100.

Mannheimer, R. and P. Natale. 2009
  L'Italia dei furbi. Milano: Il Sole 24 Ore.

Moretti E. 2012
  The New Geography of Jobs. Boston: Houghton Mifflin, Harcourt.

OECD. 2009
  How Regions Grow. Paris: OECD.

Prota F. and G. Viesti. 2012
  Senza cassa. Le politiche di sviluppo del Mezzogiorno dopo l'intervento straordinario. Bologna: il Mulino.

Putnam, R., R. Nanetti, R., and R. Leonardi. 1993
  Making Democracy Work: Civic Traditions in Modern Italy. Princeton: Princeton UP.

Rizzo, S. and G. Stella. 2007
  La casta. Milano: Rizzoli.

Rossi, R. 2008
  La politica economica italiana 1968-2007. Roma-Bari: Laterza.

Rossi, S. 2009
  Controtempo. L'Italia nella crisi mondiale, Laterza, Roma-Bari.

Stiglitz, J. 2012
  The Price of Inequality. How today's Divided Society Endangers Our Future. New York: W.W Norton & Co.

Tabellini, G. 2008
  "Tre priorità per rilanciare il paese," *Il Sole 24Ore*, 1° giugno.

Tinagli, I. 2009
  L'Italia è un paese bloccato. Muoviamoci!, Primo rapporto della Fondazione Italia Futura, www.italiafutura.it.

Tremonti, G. 2008
  La paura e la speranza. Milano: Mondadori.

Trigilia, C. 2005
  Sviluppo locale. Un progetto per l'Italia. Roma-Bari: Laterza.

Viesti, G. 2009

    Mezzogiorno a tradimento. Il Nord, il Sud e la politica che non c'è. Roma-Bari: Laterza.

Viesti, G. 2013

    Il Sud vive sulle spalle dell'Italia che produce. Falso! Roma-Bari: Laterza.

Viesti, G. and F. Prota. 2012

    1930s or 2020s? A European Grouth Strategy. Rome: IAI Working Paper 12/29.

World Bank. 2009

    World Development Report 2009: Reshaping Economic Geography. Washington: World Bank.

INDICE

ABOUT THE AUTHOR

GIANFRANCO VIESTI is Full Professor of Applied Economics at the University of Bari "Aldo Moro." His area of research is primarily dedicated to political economy on both the regional and international levels. His Italian degree is from the Bocconi University in Milan, Italy, and he was an exchange student at New York University.

He is the author of numerous books, which include: *La grande svolta. Il Mezzogiorno nell'Italia degli anni novanta*, with G. Bodo (Donzelli 1997); *Patti territoriali. Lezioni per lo sviluppo*, con P. Magnatti, F. Ramella e C. Trigilia (il Mulino 2005); *Le nuove politiche regionali dell'Unione Europea*, with F. Prota (il Mulino 2008); *Più lavoro, più talenti* (Donzelli 2010); *Senza Cassa. Le politiche di sviluppo del Mezzogiorno dopo l'intervento straordinario*, with F. Prota (il Mulino 2013); and *"Il Sud vive sulle spalle dell'Italia che produce" Falso!* (Laterza 2013). He also edited the volume, *Le sfide del cambiamento* (Donzelli 2007).

Professor Viesti has also served as a consultant for numerous international organizations that include: the Organisation for Economic Co-operation and Development (OECD), the International Labour Organisation (ILO), and the World Bank in Asia and in Latin America.

Notes

Notes

Notes

SAGGISTICA

Taking its name from the Italian – which means essays, essay writing, or nonfiction – *Saggisitca* is a referred book series dedicated to the study of all topics and cultural productions that fall under what we might consider that larger umbrella of all things Italian and Italian/American.

Vito Zagarrio
  The "Un-Happy Ending": Re-viewing The Cinema of Frank Capra.
    2011. ISBN 978-1-59954-005-4. Volume 1.
Paolo A. Giordano, Editor
  The Hyphenate Writer and The Legacy of Exile. 2010. ISBN 978-1-
    59954-007-8. Volume 2.
Dennis Barone
  America / Trattabili. 2011. ISBN 978-1-59954-018-4. Volume 3.
Fred L. Gardaphè
  The Art of Reading Italian Americana. 2011. ISBN 978-1-59954-
    019-1. Volume 4.
Anthony Julian Tamburri
  Re-viewing Italian Americana: Generalities and Specificities on Cinema. 2011. ISBN 978-1-59954-020-7. Volume 5.
Sheryl Lynn Postman
  *An Italian Writer's Journey through American Realities: Giose
    Rimanelli's English Novels. "The most tormented decade of
    America: the 60s"* ISBN 978-1-59954-034-4. Volume 6.
Luigi Fontanella
  Migrating Words: Italian Writers in the United States. 2012. ISBN
    978-1-59954-041-2. Volume 7.
Peter Covino & Dennis Barone, Editors
  Essays on Italian American Literature and Culture. 2012. ISBN
    978-1-59954-035-1. Volume 8.

  The following volume is forthcoming:
Peter Carravetta, Editor
  *Discourse Boundary Creation (LOGOS TOPOS POIESIS): A Festschrift
    in Honor of Paolo Valesio on his 70th Birthday.* ISBN 978-1-59954-036-8.

www.ingramcontent.com/pod-product-compliance
Lightning Source LLC
Chambersburg PA
CBHW032117280326
41933CB00009B/883